Quod scriptura, non iubet vetat

The Latin translates, "What is not commanded in scripture, is forbidden:'

On the Cover: Baptists rejoice to hold in common with other evangelicals the main principles of the orthodox Christian faith. However, there are points of difference and these differences are significant. In fact, because these differences arise out of God's revealed will, they are of vital importance. Hence, the barriers of separation between Baptists and others can hardly be considered a trifling matter. To suppose that Baptists are kept apart solely by their views on Baptism or the Lord's Supper is a regrettable misunderstanding. Baptists hold views which distinguish them from Catholics, Congregationalists, Episcopalians, Lutherans, Methodists, Pentecostals, and Presbyterians, and the differences are so great as not only to justify, but to demand, the separate denominational existence of Baptists. Some people think Baptists ought not teach and emphasize their differences but as E.J. Forrester stated in 1893, "Any denomination that has views which justify its separate existence, is bound to promulgate those views. If those views are of sufficient importance to justify a separate existence, they are important enough to create a duty for their promulgation ... the very same reasons which justify the separate existence of any denomination make it the duty of that denomination to teach the distinctive doctrines upon which its separate existence rests." If Baptists have a right to a separate denominational life, it is their duty to propagate their distinctive principles, without which their separate life cannot be justified or maintained.

Many among today's professing Baptists have an agenda to revise the Baptist distinctives and redefine what it means to be a Baptist. Others don't understand why it even matters. The books being reproduced in the *Baptist Distinctives Series* are republished in order that Baptists from the past may state, explain and defend the primary Baptist distinctives as they understood them. It is hoped that this Series will provide a more thorough historical perspective on what it means to be distinctively Baptist.

The Lord Jesus Christ asked, *"And why call ye me, Lord, Lord, and do not the things which I say?"* (Luke 6:46). The immediate context surrounding this question explains what it means to be a true disciple of Christ. Addressing the same issue, Christ's question is meant to show that a confession of discipleship to the Lord Jesus Christ is inconsistent and untrue if it is not accompanied with a corresponding submission to His authoritative commands. Christ's question teaches us that a true recognition of His authority as Lord inevitably includes a submission to the authority of His Word. Hence, with this question Christ has made it forever impossible to separate His authority as King from the authority of His Word. These two principles—the authority of Christ as King and the authority of His Word—are the two most fundamental Baptist distinctives. The first gives rise to the second and out of these two all the other Baptist distinctives emanate. As F.M. Iams wrote in 1894, "Loyalty to Christ as King, manifesting itself in a constant and unswerving obedience to His will as revealed in His written Word, is the real source of all the Baptist distinctives:' In the search for the *primary* Baptist distinctive many have settled on the Lordship of Christ as the most basic distinctive. Strangely, in doing this, some have attempted to separate Christ's Lordship from the authority of Scripture, as if you could embrace Christ's authority without submitting to what He commanded. However, while Christ's Lordship and Kingly authority can be isolated and considered essentially for discussion's sake, we see from Christ's own words in Luke 6:46 that His Lordship is really inseparable from His Word and, with regard to real Christian discipleship, there can be no practical submission to the one without a practical submission to the other.

In the symbol above the Kingly Crown and the Open Bible represent the inseparable truths of Christ's Kingly and Biblical authority. The Crown and Bible graphics are supplemented by three Bible verses (Ecclesiastes 8:4, Matthew 28:18-20, and Luke 6:46) that reiterate and reinforce the inextricable connection between the authority of Christ as King and the authority of His Word. The truths symbolized by these components are further emphasized by the Latin quotation - *quod scriptura, non iubet vetat*— i.e., "What is not commanded in scripture, is forbidden:' This Latin quote has been considered historically as a summary statement of the regulative principle of Scripture. Together these various symbolic components converge to exhibit the two most foundational Baptist Distinctives out of which all the other Baptist Distinctives arise. Consequently, we have chosen this composite symbol as a logo to represent the primary truths set forth in the *Baptist Distinctives Series.*

THE PRICE

OF

SOUL-LIBERTY

AND WHO PAID IT

HENRY CLAY FISH
1820-1877

THE PRICE

OF

SOUL-LIBERTY

AND WHO PAID IT

BY

HENRY C. FISH, D.D.

———

"Freedom of Conscience, unlimited freedom of mind, was, from the
first, the trophy of the Baptists." —George Bancroft.

———

The Baptist Standard Bearer, Inc.

NUMBER ONE IRON OAKS DRIVE • PARIS, ARKANSAS 72855

Thou hast given a *standard* to them that fear thee;
that it may be displayed because of the truth.
-- *Psalm 60:4*

Reprinted in 2008

by

THE BAPTIST STANDARD BEARER, INC.

No. 1 Iron Oaks Drive
Paris, Arkansas 72855
(479) 963-3831

THE WALDENSIAN EMBLEM
lux lucet in tenebris
"The Light Shineth in the Darkness"

ISBN-10: 1579786022
ISBN-13: 9781579786021

Preface to the 1983 Reprint

The first murder in history was on the ground of religious difference. Cains often murder Abels. Those with divine favor are always hated by those who refuse the grace of God. In all ages and in all cultures, men have shown themselves more willing to persecute others on the ground of religious dissent than for any other single reason.

Issues of religious liberty proliferate on every hand. Devotees of modern cults are being deprogrammed, sometimes against their will. In some states, magistrates are usurping authority over the parents of Christian day-school students in attempts to force them to return to the public school. In their attempts to disseminate the truth, many Christian radio broadcasters are in constant friction with the FCC. One of the greatest challenges of our time seems to be the totalitarian state's claim to have absolute rights over the individual conscience. Thus, we are happy to see the reappearance of this book by Henry Fish. It will surely prove timely for any pertinent discussion of contemporary church-state issues.

Man was created to be different from the other creatures. Only he was made in the divine image. Only he had a will. He could reason and make decisions. Unlike the birds in the air which were programmed to fly and unlike the fish in the ocean which were programmed to swim, man was not programmed. He had the power of choice.

This was his greatest glory...and the most expensive part of creation, for it cost God His Son. When man fell into sin, however, his will became enslaved so that he could no longer choose God. Decision-making was still possible, even hard and difficult ones based on high moral and ethical principles, but the *Imago Dei* was effaced. Here, in Henry Fish's reprinted book, we are reminded that man's tarnished image has often expressed itself in religious bigotry.

Three hundred years ago, Louis Du Moulin wrote these words:

> A particular person, or church, ought not to submit their faith, their religion, nor the guidance of their manners to an authority which is subject to error, but only to the Word of God, which is an infallible authority.

Even before that, Robert Brown, in his book *Reformation Without Tarrying for Any,* said:

> The Lord's people is of the willing sort...for it is the conscience and not the power of man that will drive it to seek the Lord's kingdom.

Neither of these writers was a Baptist in a strict sense of the term, but both of them shared the views later made famous by many Baptist authors. In 1614, Leonard Bushar wrote a tract entitled *Religious Peace, or a Plea for a Liberty of Conscience.* The following year, an obscure member of Thomas Helwy's church wrote a book named *Persecution for Religion Judged and Condemned.* Samuel Richardson, a member of a Particular Baptist church in London, authored a book entitled *The Necessity of Toleration in Matters of Religion* (1647). Another book appeared in 1660, *The Humble Petition and Representation of the Sufferings of Several Peaceable and Innocent Subjects, called by the Name of Anabaptists...for the Testimony of*

Our Good Conscience. The next year, John Sturgion wrote a pamphlet called *A Plea for Toleration of Opinion and Persuasion in Matters of Religion...Showing the Unreasonableness of Prescribing to Other Men's Faith and the Evil of Persecuting Different Opinions.* Greatest of them all was Roger Williams' publication called *The Bloody Tenent of Persecution,* which appeared in 1644. The ideas in this monumental effort would be perpetuated as part of the American Constitution in Article I of the Bill of Rights.

Baptist views on soul-liberty are in marked contrast to Roman Catholic and Protestant concepts. Ann Freemantle, in her book, *The Papal Encyclicals,* has reprinted many of the modern papal statements including some which denounce liberty of conscience. One 19th century pope called religious liberty "insanity." The reformers were not far behind. In 1885, a statue was erected in the city of Zurich to honor Zwingli. The great reformer is shown with a Bible in one hand and a sword in the other, symbolizing the civil power in unholy alliance with ecclesiastical power. Similar statues could have been erected to Martin Luther in Germany, John Calvin in Geneva, John Knox in Scotland, Thomas Cranmer in England, and John Cotton in New England. All of them believed as Augistine did, namely, that God has two hands by which He administers the affairs of this world. One hand is the church; the other is the magistrate. Just as one hand must help the other in normal bodily functions, so the church and the state must help each other as God performs His task in human history.

Protestant confessions of faith from the 16th and 17th centuries gave the magistrate a coercive power in religious affairs. Even the most venerable statement coming out of the Westminster Assembly of 1647 stated that religious dissenters should be "lawfully called to account, and proceeded against by the censures of the Church, and by the power of the Civil Magistrate." Thus, the state was to help enforce the law against deviations of worship. Many of the Presbyterian members of the Westminster Assembly published books against religious liberty. Ephraim Pagitt, Richard Byfield, Adam Stewart, and Samuel Rutherford were only a few of the many. Separation of church and state was missing from all of their writings. Neither in the 16th nor 17th centuries do we find the reformers or their children exhibiting much tolerance of religious dissent.

Luther and Calvin believed in magisterial force. The former said: "Since it is not good that in one parish the people should be exposed to contradictory preaching, he (the magistrate) should order to be silent whatever does not consist with the Scriptures." Calvin agreed: "Godly princes may issue edicts for compelling obstinate and religious persons to worship the true God and to maintain the unity of the faith." In 1520, Martin Luther had written his famous tract entitled *Liberty of the Christian Man,* but within a very few years he was urging the nobility of the land to use force against the Baptists.

From such seed plots many theocratic notions have sprung. A famous law against religious dissent was adopted in Massachusetts in 1644. Baptists were sentenced to banishment. One of the New England leaders, John Cotton, wrote that "toleration made the world anti-Christian."

Eventually the history of religious bigotry was going to change, however. In the United States, church and state were finally separated by the Bill of Rights. Two of the thirteen colonies displayed Baptist influence in the forefront of this struggle. Rhode Island had as its founder Roger Williams, ensuring the adoption of religious toleration from the very beginning. In Pennsylvania, William Penn, also influenced by Baptist beliefs, was another who espoused religious liberty.

Basic concepts of soul-liberty can be found in all the great Baptist confessions such as the Schleitheim Confession (1527), the London Confession (1644), the General Baptist Confession (1660), the Orthodox Creed (1678), and the New Hampshire Confession (1833). These all reveal that Baptists have spoken with a united voice regarding the great principle of soul-liberty.

Many modern fundamentalist leaders have continued to drink at the theocratic well which was dug by ancients from Augustine to Luther and beyond. John Cotton was not the only one who equated the American experiment with the Old Testament economy of Israel in order to erect a modern counterpart of Manifest Destiny. Our founding fathers separated church and state, but ideas of civil religion have persisted through the two hundred years of our history. A study of the material in Henry C. Fish's book will undoubtedly prove to be of great interest to those who are caught in the theocratic web of modern Christian political activism.

It is time that Baptists did some serious thinking about this great principle of soul-liberty, independent thinking which is not encumbered by four hundred years of theocratic Protestant tradition. Although Baptists were condemned by Roman Catholics and Protestants alike, yet today they are behaving like the reformers in many current church-state activities. Indeed, theirs has been the only denomination in all of church history which has consistently denied the use of magisterial force to accomplish spiritual ends. Only in modern times has this principle been called into question.

Western civilization is surely indebted to our Baptist forefathers for giving clear testimony to the advantage of the separation of church and state. Augustine viewed the church and the state as coexistent. Much error resulted as the church then has the power of capital punishment. For a thousand years throughout the Middle Ages this was the opinion of the papal church. Sixteenth-century Anabaptists such as Dietrich Philips, Menno Simons, and Henry Jacob all parted company with Augustine's philosophy. They wrote against the equation of Israel and the church. By doing so, they established a new basis for soul-liberty. Later on, covenant theology came into being as a result of the work of Cocceius in the middle of the 17th century. Covenant theology has proven to be a very weak basis on which to establish the great doctrine of individual conscience. Protestants who have been most involved with covenant theology need to reread the writings of Isaac Backus and Roger Williams, who parted company with theocratic tendencies in the interest of maintaining the great Baptist principle of religious liberty.

We welcome this new edition of Henry Fish's book on soul-liberty. Evangelical discussion of church-state relationships will be more sharply focused because of its reappearance.

Rembert B. Carter, M.Div., Ph.D.
Professor of History
Baptist Bible College of Pennsylvania

AUTHOR'S PREFACE

Upon the subject treated in the following pages, there is little room for originality; since almost every thing brought forward must necessarily be gleaned from the writings of those who have gone before us.

At the same time, it is believed that nowhere else are exhibited so fully and authoritatively (certainly not in the same compass,) the facts bearing upon the struggles and triumphs of RELIGIOUS LIBERTY, especially in these United States.

These facts ought to be known by each succeeding generation of Christians. Church members, generally, should be in possession of them; the children in our Sunday Schools should become familiar with them; and converts added to the Churches should know how dearly purchased, by our fathers, are the privileges which they enjoy.

It has been justly said, that without a strong regard to the history and the principles of their ancestors, a denomination may quite lose sight of those distinctive peculiarities which have been the source of its usefulness.

The hope is entertained, therefore, that the humble mission of this little volume will be one of usefulness.

NEWARK, June 7, 1860.

CONTENTS

SOUL-LIBERTY

SOUL-LIBERTY is the liberty to think and act in religious matters without human dictation or control.

The people of this country, and of some other parts of the world, now enjoy this privilege; but the time was when it was denied them.

The chief captain said to Paul, "With a great price I obtained this freedom." So may we say, with respect to religious freedom. The price of it was great; a price paid in tears, and toils, and blood.

But who paid this price? We ought to know, for how else shall we appreciate this great blessing, and cherish, as we ought, the memory of those who suffered to procure it?

It is a remark of the great American historian, Bancroft, that "Freedom of conscience, unlimited freedom of mind, was from the first, the trophy of the BAPTISTS."

This is a just remark; and it is the purpose of this little book, to furnish some of these deeply interesting facts upon which such an assertion is based.

It is not denied that religious liberty has had noble champions of a different faith; but its main, and chief, and foremost advocates have been among the Baptists.

This would be naturally expected, for two reasons: First, from their peculiarity of belief. The distinguishing tenet of this denomination is, *direct personal and individual responsibility to God.* With them it is a fundamental doctrine, that no man has a right to dictate to another in religion; to control the action of his conscience, or to compel him to any creed or form of worship against his will. Everything pertaining to religion, must be a matter of *intelligent conviction and voluntary choice.* To God each man, for himself, either stands or falls. As Paul has it, "Who art thou that judgest another man's servant. To his own master he standeth or falleth."

Or, as it is expressed in the familiar couplet:

> "Consciences and souls were made
> To be the Lord's alone."

Hence the Baptists never baptize infants. Besides wanting, as they believe, the support of the Scriptures, it impinges upon this matter of voluntary religious action. It deprives the child of the liberty of deciding *for himself* as to what is obedience to a certain Gospel command, and performing, for himself, intelligently, a duty enjoined upon all true believers. He is under engagements, when he grows up, in the forming of which engagements, he had no voluntary agency.

And declining interference as to the *child's* freedom, the Baptists, would, of course, resist it in respect to the adult.

The other reason why it might be expected that the

Baptists would be the foremost defenders of religious freedom, is, because they have suffered most from religious intolerance and oppression. Other denominations have suffered something — they *much.* The period of their suffering has been long.

In every age of the Christian era, there have been those holding their views; and they have always been subject to some degree of suffering for holding them.

The fourth century had not passed, when the doctrine of *sacramental efficacy* came to be a prevailing opinion. Baptism was considered the medium of grace; and without it, there could be no salvation. Hence arose "clinic," or sick-room baptism; as also that of unconscious children. Against this practice some protested, declaring that it was a perversion of the original design of the ordinance, which in such cases was not valid.

The protesting party were denounced and assailed. In the year 413 re-baptism, as it was termed, was forbidden throughout the Roman Empire, under the penalty of death.

In the following year, the council of Carthage, of which Augustine was the President, thus decreed: "We will that whosoever denies that little children, by baptism, are freed from perdition and eternally saved, that they be accursed." Justinian, in the beginning of the sixth century, ordered new-born babes to be baptized, under a penalty for neglecting it.

To whom these acts referred, it is not difficult to perceive.

Thus early did Baptists begin to pay the price of Soul-Liberty. And, ever suffering for their faith, is it strange

that they should have been first and foremost in denouncing religious tyranny, and proclaiming the sancti-
ty of conscience?

I.

A PEEP INTO THE EARLY AGES.

Some may doubt that there *were* Baptists in the early ages. It will be well, therefore, to verify what has been said above, as to the existence of Baptists in primitive times, and their pleas for Soul-Liberty. Within the present century the King of Holland selected his chaplain, Dr. J. J. Dermont, and Dr. Ypeig, professor of theology at the University of Groningen, both of the Dutch Reformed Church, to draw up a history of the Dutch Baptists. In the authentic volume which they prepared and published at Breda, in 1819, they arrived at the following deliberate conclusions:

"We have now seen that the Baptists, who were formerly called Anabaptists, and in later times Mennonites, were the original Waldenses, and who, long in the history of the Church, received the honor of that origin. On this account, *the Baptists may be considered as the only Christian community which has stood since the days of the Apostles,* and as a Christian society which has *preserved pure the doctrines of the Gospel through all ages.* The perfectly correct external and internal economy of the Baptist denomination tends to confirm the truth, disputed by the Romish Church, that the Reformation brought about in the sixteenth century, was in the highest degree necessary, and at the same time *goes to refute the erroneous notion of the Catholics that their communion is the most ancient."*

This is very strong testimony; but let us look farther. The Donatists, who held many of the views of the Baptists, and who had their origin as a distinct sect in the year 311, were distinguished for their "ideas concerning *liberty of conscience;* concerning the *rights of free religious conviction."** With these Donatists is to be found, according to Neander, "the true historical origin of the Waldenses."†

Much has been written, of late, to disprove any connection of the ancient Baptists of Germany with the Waldensian Christians. But Limborch, whose account of them Dr. Wall endorses as the most reliable, says: "The Waldenses appear to have been plain men, unskilful and inexperienced, and if their opinions and customs were to be examined without prejudice, it would appear that among all the modern sects of Christians, *they bear the greatest resemblance to the Mennonites,"* or modern Dutch Baptists.‡

And Dr. Mosheim, the great Church historian says: "Before the rise of Luther and Calvin, there lay concealed in almost all the countries of Europe, persons

* Neander's History of Christian Religion,
  Vol. II., pages 182-217. Torrey.

† *Ibid.*

‡ History of Inquisition, Vol. II., page 230.

who adhered tenaciously to the principles of the modern Dutch Baptists."

There is still extant among the remains left by these most ancient Christians, a Treatise on Anti-Christ, which is an authentic exposition of their faith; dating back, as is generally supposed, to about the year 1120; but Neander thinks it much older. It thus describes Anti-Christ: "He arrived at maturity when men whose hearts were set upon the world multiplied in the Church, *and by the union of Church and State, got the power of both into their hands*... He teaches to *baptize children* into the faith, and attributes to this the work of regeneration, thus confounding the work of the Holy Spirit in regeneration with the external of baptism: and on this foundation bestows orders, and indeed grounds all his Christianity." They farther declare, "We hold in abhorrence all human inventions as proceeding from Anti-Christ, which produce distrust, and are prejudicial to the *liberty of the mind.*" Here are clearly presented some of the cardinal opinions of the Baptists: such as regeneration by the Holy Spirit, individual belief as necessary to baptism, and the independence of the Church, as separate from the State. And this was at least some *seven hundred years* ago;—perhaps long before.

From this time forward, we find men protesting warmly, at the same time, against two things, viz., *compulsion in religion* and *infant baptism.* As examples, reference may be made to the Petrobrussians (1110), the Henririans (1140), Arnold of Brescia (1136-57), who was condemned by Pope Innocent II *as an opponent of infant baptism,* and Peter Auteru (about 1300), who also protested against the practice referred to.

Mosheim says of the Mennonites, or Dutch Baptists, who sprang from the Waldenses in 1536, that the basis of all their peculiarities is, "That the kingdom which Christ has established on earth, *is a visible society or company in which is no place for any but holy or pious persons."*

In 1540, the Waldenses thus declare against priestly authority and infant Church membership: "Our Lord Jesus Christ did *not take upon himself any jurisdiction of temporal power."...*"By baptism we are received into the holy congregation of God's people, *previously possessing and declaring our faith and change of life."*

From the facts now sumbitted, it is plain that all through the early ages there were those who held, substantially, the Baptist faith. And what these faithful witnesses to the "truth as it is in Jesus" suffered, eternity alone will reveal.

Church and State were leagued in unholy embrace, and opinions and practices at variance with the declared standards were punishable by the civil power with the severest penalties. Mention may be made, in illustration, of the seven Baptists in Holland, who were imprisoned, in 1523, and two of them *burned;* the putting to death of ten, shortly after; and of fourteen others, still, not long afterwards; the sixteen men who were beheaded at Delft, when fifteen women were drowned for their faith, while twenty-seven others had, just before, on that same spot, laid down their lives for their belief; and of Jerome of Prague, also a Baptist, who, when bound to the stake with wet cords and iron chain, while the faggots were inclosing him breast-high, cried out to the officer, "Bring hither thy torch! Perform thy office before my face! Had I feared death, I might have avoided it!" And of Felix Manth, who *denied infant baptism*, and, as Zwingle said, *wished to form churches free from sin;* and who, being sentenced, in 1526, to be drowned for this heresy, sung with a loud voice, as he lay bound upon the hurdle, ready to be tossed into the stream, "Into thy hands, O Lord, I commend my spirit!" And of the learned and eloquent Hubmeyer, who, for his Baptist opinions, was burnt in 1528, while his devoted wife was drowned in the Danube, for a like offense.*

Mention may also be made of Hans Kaeffer and Leonard Freek, who for opposing infant baptism were beheaded at Schevos, in Germany, in 1528, two other men, for the same offence, and in the same year, being beheaded at Augsburg. And of the forty-three persons, who were burned, for a like offence, at Saltzburg and

---

*It is common to allege that the Anabaptists, as they were styled—Baptizers *again*— suffered because they were wild errorists and insurrectionists. With some grains of allowance, these charges are highly unjust. Their enemies and persecutors, and prejudiced writers, have been their historians. The time is coming when it will be seen that thousands of the choicest spirits of any age, have shared in the common opprobrium of the "Madmen of Munster." As a high authority, Bayle, in his Historical and Critical Dictionary, in the notes to his article on the Anabaptists, besides suggesting numerous interesting points of inquiry, furnishes decisive testimony in favor of many who went under that name. "It is certain," says he, "that many Anabaptists, who suffered death for their opinions, had no thoughts of making an insurrection."

Waltzen, also in the same year. And of the *three hundred and fifty* put to death at Altre, Germany, in 1529, for their denial of the same practice; — the men mostly being beheaded, and the women drowned. And of the three men who, in 1533, at Harlem, were chained to a post, and then roasted by a fire at a distance until they died.

What multitudes of Baptists had, before this, become Martyrs, may be conjectured from what occurred at the Reformation, when they were counted by tens, and even by hundreds of thousands. The free cities of Europe generally — the Italian Republics of the Middle Ages, — the Moors in Spain — and the princes of Provence, or Southern France, — all these, at times, for long periods, says an able church historian, gave protection to the persecuted Baptists, who were known alike by their original name of Cathari, the *pure*, and by the subsequent names of Paulicians, Paterines, and poor men of Lyons, down to the beginning of the twelfth century.

A striking picture of the persecutions for conscience above referred to, is furnished in the case of Elizabeth, for a while a Beguin nun, who, for embracing the true Gospel, was apprehended in the year 1549.

The narrative of her trial, as it comes down to us, is deeply interesting.

When the officers came to the house where she lived, they found a Latin New Testament. Having apprehended this holy woman, they said, "We have the right person, — we have now the teacher;" and asked, "Where is your husband? Where is Menno Simon?" etc. They conveyed her to the council-house, and the next day two white capuchin friars conducted her to another place, where she was brought before the council. She was asked by them, on oath, whether she had a husband. Her reply was, "It is not permitted us to swear; but our words must be yea, yea, and nay, nay. I have no husband."

Council. We say that you are a teacher, who mislead many, and this we have been told concerning you by others. We wish to know who are your friends.

Elizabeth. My God has commanded me to love the Lord my God, and, therefore, to honor my parents. I will not therefore tell you who are my parents; for to suffer for Christ's name is (in the esteem of the public) to the dishonor of my friends.

Coun. On this we will not further press you, but we would know what people you have taught.

Eliz. Oh, no, gentlemen, excuse me herein, and ask me concerning my faith; that I will most readily confess.

Coun. We shall use such severe means as will make you confess.

Eliz. I trust, through the grace of God, that he will keep my tongue, so that I shall not become a traitor, and deliver my brother to death.

Coun. What persons were present when you were baptized?

Eliz. Christ said "Ask those that were present, or that heard it."

Coun. Now we see that you are a teacher; for you wish to make yourself like Christ.

Eliz. No, gentlemen, God forbid I should; for I esteem myself no better than the sweepings of the house of the Lord.

Coun. What then do you hold concerning the house of

God? Do you not consider our Church to be the house of God?

Eliz. No, indeed, gentlemen; for it is written, "Ye are the temple of the living God;" as God says, "I will dwell in them, and walk in them."

Coun. What do you think of our mass?

Eliz. I do not approve of your mass; but whatever agrees with God's word, that I highly esteem.

Coun. What do you think of the most holy sacrament?

Eliz. I have never in my life read in Holy Scripture of a holy sacrament; but I have read of the Supper of the Lord. (Here she repeated the Scriptures which referred to this ordinance.)

Coun. Be silent; for the devil speaks by your mouth.

Eliz. This indeed, gentlemen, is but a small matter; for the servant is no better than his Lord.

Coun. You speak with a proud spirit.

Eliz. No, gentlemen, I speak with freedom of spirit.

Coun. What did the Lord say when he gave the Supper to his disciples?

Eliz. What did he give them, flesh or bread?

Coun. He gave them bread.

Eliz. Did not the Lord then continue sitting there? Who then could eat the Lord's flesh?

Coun. What do you hold concerning infant baptism, that you should have had yourself baptized again?

Eliz. No, gentlemen; I have not been baptized again; I was baptized *once*, on my own confession of faith; for it is written that baptism belongs to believers.

Coun. Are our children then lost, because they have been baptized?

Eliz. No, gentlemen; far be it from me that I should condemn the children.

Coun. Do you not expect salvation from baptism?

Eliz. No, gentlemen; all the waters in the sea cannot save me; but salvation is in Christ; and he has commanded me to love the Lord my God above all things, and my neighbor as myself.

Coun. Have the priests power to forgive sins?

Eliz. No, gentlemen; how can I believe that? I say that Christ is the only priest through whom is the forgiveness of sins.

Coun. You say that you believe all that agrees with the Holy Scriptures; do you then agree with the words of James?

Eliz. Yes, truly, gentlemen. How could I not agree with them?

Coun. Has he not said, "Go to the elder of the Church, that he may anoint you, and pray for you?"

Eliz. Yes, gentlemen. Do you then mean to say that you are of *such* a Church?

Coun. The Holy Ghost has already *saved* you; you need neither confession nor sacrament.

Eliz. No, gentlemen. I acknowledge, indeed, that I have transgressed the command of the Pope, which has been confirmed by the Emperor's proclamation. But show me any article in which I have transgressed against the Lord my God, and I will say, "Woe is me, poor miserable creature!"

This is recorded as the first confession. She was afterwards brought again before the Council, and lead into the torture tower, the executioner, Hans, being present.

The Council then said: "We have thus far proceeded with mildness, and if you will not confess, we will treat you with severity."

The procurer-general spoke,—"Master Hans, lay hold of her." Hans answered, "Oh, no, gentlemen, she will confess voluntarily:" and as she would not make a voluntary confession, he put thumb-screws on both her thumbs and fore-fingers, so that the blood sprang out of her nails.

Elizabeth exclaimed, "Oh, I cannot longer bear it." The Council said, "Confess, and we will ease your pain." But she cried to the Lord her God, "Help, O my God, thy poor handmaid: thou art a helper in time of need."

The Council cried out, "Confess, and we will ease your pain; for we spoke to you of confessing, and not of calling on God the Lord." But she continued steadfastly calling upon the Lord her God.

And the Lord relieved her pain, so that she said to the council, "Ask me, and I will answer you; for I feel no longer any pain in my body as before."

Coun. Will you not yet confess?

Eliz. No, gentlemen.

They then put two terrible iron screws upon her ankles. She said, "Oh, gentlemen, put me not to shame." The procurer-general said, "No, Miss Elizabeth, we shall not treat you improperly." She then fainted; and they said one to another, "Perhaps she is dead." Coming to herself, she said, "I am alive, and not dead." They then loosed all the iron screws, and spoke to her with entreaties.

Eliz. Why do you thus entreat me? They deal so with children.

Thus they could not draw from her a word to the injury of her associates in the Lord, or of any individual.

Coun. Will you recant all the things you have before confessed?

Eliz. No, indeed, gentlemen; but I will seal them with my blood.

Coun. We will no longer distress you, if you will now freely tell us who it was that baptized you.

Eliz. Oh, no, gentlemen; I have already told you that I will not confess that to you.

After this, the sentence was pronounced upon her, March 27, 1549, and she was condemned to death, and drowned in a sack. Thus she willingly offered her body a living sacrifice unto God. Her enemies showed the extent of their hatred; happily, however, their real power was but small, for though her body was committed to the river, her happy spirit was soon filled with the triumphant joys of the upper world.

In one of the Mennonite hymn-books it is to be read, a hymn descriptive of the cloister life, which is said to have been composed by Elizabeth, and handed down from one generation to another, till printed in 1618. It consists of forty-eight verses, with the following refrain or chorus: —

> "In thanks to God will I delight,
> And love and praise with all my might,
> Honor and fear Him day and night."*

Behold, reader, in this deeply affecting picture of a scene transacted three hundred years ago, the PRICE OF SOUL-LIBERTY, AND WHO PAID IT! Behold what it *cost,*

* See Baptist Martyrs, p. 154.

once, to maintain those principles, which may now be held in many parts of the world without molestation.

We have already referred, in several instances, to the Waldensian Baptists, and to their having been subjects of persecution for their religious opinions and practices. Let us gather another illustration or two of our subject, from this interesting people.

II.

SOUL-LIBERTY AMONG THE WALDENSES.

About the year 1400, says Jones, the church historian, a violent outrage was committed upon the Waldenses who inhabited the valley of Pragela, in Peidmont, by the Catholic party resident in that neighborhood. The attack, which seems to have been of the most furious kind, was made towards the end of the month of December, when the mountains were covered with snow, and thereby rendered so difficult of access, that the peaceable inhabitants of the valleys, were wholly unapprised that such an attempt was meditated; and the persecutors were in actual possession of their caves, before the former seem to have been aware of any hostile designs against them. In this pitiable plight they had recourse to the only alternative which remained for saving their lives, — they fled to one of the highest mountains of the Alps, with their wives and children, the unhappy mothers carrying the cradle in one hand, and in the other, leading such of their offspring as were able to walk.

Their inhuman invaders, whose feet were swift to shed blood, pursued them in their flight, until night came on, and slew great numbers of them before they could reach the mountains. Those that escaped were, however, reserved to experience a fate not more enviable.

Overtaken by the shades of night, they wandered up and down the mountains, covered with snow, destitute of the means of shelter from the inclemencies of the weather, or of supporting themselves under it by any of the comforts which Providence has destined for that purpose. Benumbed with cold, they fell an easy prey to the severity of the climate; and when the night had passed away, there were found by their cradles, or lying upon the snow, *fourscore of their infants*, deprived of life, many of the mothers also lying dead by their sides, and others just upon the point of expiring. During the nights, their enemies were busily employed in plundering the houses of everything that was valuable, which they conveyed away to Susa. A poor woman, belonging to the Waldenses, named Margaret Athode, was next morning found hanging upon a tree.

In 1487, a lieutenant and his troops came against the people of the valley of Loyse. The inhabitants, apprised of their approach, fled into their caves at the tops of the mountains, carrying with them their children, and whatever valuables they had, as well as what was thought necessary for their support and nourishment. The lieutenant, finding the inhabitants all fled, and that not an individual appeared with whom he could converse, at length discovered their retreats, and causing quantities of wood to be placed at their entrances, ordered it to be set on fire. The consequence was, that *four hundred chil-*

dren were suffocated in their cradles, or in the arms of
their dead mothers, while multitudes, to avoid dying by
suffocation, or being burnt to death, precipitated themselves headlong from their caverns upon the rocks be-
low, where they were dashed to pieces; or if any escaped
death by the fall, they were immediately slaughtered by
the brutal soldiery.

"It is held as unquestionably true," says Perrin,
"amongst the Waldenses dwelling in the adjacent valleys, that more than *three thousand persons,* men and
women, belonging to the valley of Loyse, perished on
this occasion. And, indeed, they were wholly extermi-
nated, for the valley was afterwards peopled with new
inhabitants; not one family of the Waldenses having
subsequently resided in it; which proves beyond dis-
pute, that all the inhabitants, and of both sexes, died at
that time."*

On the 25th of January, 1655, a public document appeared, which has since been but too well known by the
title of "The Order of Gastaldo." Thus runs the pre-
amble: "Andrew Gastaldo, Doctor of the Civil Law, Master Auditor Ordinary, sitting in the most illustrious
Chamber of Accounts of his royal highness, and Conser-
vator-General of the holy faith, for the observation of
the orders published against the pretended reformed
religion of the valley of Lucerne, Perouse, and St. Martino, and upon this account especially deputed by his
said royal highness."

After stating the authority which had been vested in
him by the Duke, on the 13th of the same month, it pro-
* Perrin's History, book ii., chap. 3.

ceeds "to command and enjoin every head of a family, with its members, of the reformed religion, of whatever rank, degree, or condition soever, without exception, inhabiting or possessing estates in the places of Lucerne, Lucernetta, S. Glovanni, La Torre, Bubbiana, *within three days after the publication of these presents, to withdraw and to depart, and to be, with their families, withdrawn out of the said places, and transported into the places allowed by his royal highness, during his good pleasure, etc., under pain of death and confiscation of houses and goods; provided always that they do not make it appear to us within twenty days following, that they are become Catholics,* or that they have sold their goods to the Catholics. Furthermore, his royal highness intends, and wills, that in the places, (to which they were to transport themselves,) the holy mass shall be celebrated in every one of them; and that for any persons of the said reformed religion to molest, either in deed or word, the missionary fathers, and those that attend them, much less to divert or dissuade any one of the said religion from turning Catholic, he shall do it on pain of death, etc."

It is not difficult to conjecture, says the narrator, what must have been the distress and misery consequent upon a compliance with such an order as this, and more especially in such a country as Piedmont, at such a season of the year. Thousands of families, comprehending the aged and infirm, the sick and afflicted, the delicate female and the helpless infant—all compelled to abandon their homes in the very depth of winter, in a country where the snow is visible upon the tops of the mountains, throughout every month of the year. All this surely presents a picture of distress sufficient to rend the heart.

On the first issuing of this edict, the Waldenses sent deputies to the governor of the province, humbly representing to him the unreasonableness and cruelty of this command. They stated the absolute impossibility of so many souls finding subsistence in the places to which they were ordered to transport themselves; the countries scarcely affording adequate supply for their present inhabitants. To which they added, that this command was expressly contrary to all their rights, as the peaceable subject of his highness, and the concessions which had been uniformly granted them, of maintaining, without molestation, their religious profession. But the inhuman governor refused to pay the least attention to their application. Disappointed in this, they next begged time to present their humble supplication to his royal highness. But even this boon was refused them, unless they would allow him to draw up their petition and prescribe the form of it. Finding that what he proposed was equally inimical to their rights and consciences, they declined his proposal. They now found that the only alternative which remained for them was to abandon their houses and properties, and to retire, with their families, their wives and children, aged parents and helpless infants, the halt, the lame and the blind, to traverse the country, through the rain, snow and ice, encompassed with a thousand difficulties.

> "The world was all before them, whence to choose
> Their place of rest, and Providence their guide."

But these things were only the beginning of sorrows,

to this afflicted people. For no sooner had they quitted their houses, than a banditti broke into them, pillaging and plundering whatever they had left behind. They next proceeded to raze their habitations to the ground, to cut down the trees and turn the neighborhood into a desolate wilderness; and all this without the least remonstrance from Gastaldo. These things, however, were only a trifle in comparison to what followed.

But the reader will best learn this sad story from the parties who were interested in this melancholy catastrophe; and the following is a copy of the letter which some of the survivors wrote to their Christain friends, in distant countries, as soon as the tragedy was over:

"Brethren and Fathers!

"Our tears are no more of water but of blood, which not only obscure our sight, but oppress our very hearts. Our pen is guided by a trembling hand, and our minds distracted by such unexpected alarms, that we are incapable of framing a letter which shall correspond with our wishes, or the strangeness of our desolations. In this respect, therefore, we plead your excuse, and that you would endeavor to collect our meaning from what we would impart to you.

"Whatever reports may have been circulated concerning our obstinacy in refusing to have recourse to his royal highness for a redress of our heavy grievances and molestations, you cannot but know that we have never desisted from writing supplicatory letters, or presenting our humble requests, by the hands of our deputies, and that they were sent and referred, sometimes to the council 'de propaganda fide,'* at other times to the Marquis of Pionessa,† and that the three last times they were positively rejected, and refused so much as an audience, under the pretext that they had no credentials nor instructions, which should authorize them to promise or accept, on the behalf of their respective churches, whatever it might please his highness to grant or bestow upon them.

"And by the instigation and contrivance of the Roman clergy, there was secretly placed in ambush an army of six thousand men, who, animated and encouraged thereto by the personal presence and active exertions of the Marquis of Pionessa, fell suddenly, and in the most violent manner, upon the inhabitants of S. Giovanni and La Torre.

"This army having once entered and got a footing, was soon augmented by the addition of a multitude of the neighboring inhabitants throughout all Piedmont, who hearing that we were given up as a prey to the plunderers, fell upon the poor people with impetuous fury. To all those were added an incalculable number of persons that had been outlawed, prisoners, and other offenders, who expected thereby to have saved their souls and filled their purses. And the better to effect their

---

* A council established by the court of Rome, for propagating the faith, or, in plain English, for extirpating heretics.

† This unfeeling man seems to have sustained the station of prime-minister in the court of the Duke of Savoy, and commander-in-chief of his army.

purposes, the inhabitants were compelled to receive five or six regiments of the French army, besides some Irish, to whom, it is reported, our country was promised, with several troops of vagabond persons, under the pretext of coming into the valleys for fresh quarters.

"This great multitude, by virtue of a license from the Marquis of Pionessa, instigated by the monks, and enticed and conducted by our wicked and unnatural neighbors, attacked us with such violence on every side, especially in Angrogne, Villaro, and Bobbio; and in a manner so horribly treacherous, that in an instant all was one entire scene of confusion, and the inhabitants, after a fruitless skirmish to defend themselves, were compelled to flee for their lives, with their wives and children; and that not merely the inhabitants of the plain, but those of the mountains also. Nor was all their diligence sufficient to prevent the destruction of a very considerable number of them. For in many places such as Villaro and Bobbio, they were so hemmed in on every side, the army having seized on the fort of Mareburgh, and by that means blocked up the avenue, that there remained no possibility of escape, and nothing remained for them but to be massacred and put to death.

"In one place they mercilessly tortured not less than a hundred and fifty women and their children, chopping off the heads of some, and dashing the brains of others against the rocks. And in regard to those whom they took prisoners from fifteen years old and upwards, who refused to go to mass, they hanged some, and nailed others to the trees by the feet with their heads downwards. It is reported that they carried some persons of note prisoners to Turin, viz., our poor brother and pastor, Mr. Gros, with some part of his family. In short, there is neither cattle nor provisions of any kind left in the valley of Lucerne. It is but too evident that all is lost, since there are some whole districts, especially S. Giovanni and La Torre, where the business of setting fire to our houses and churches was so dexterously managed, by a Franciscan friar and a certain priest, that they left not so much as one of either unburnt. In these desolations, the mother has been bereft of her dear child; the husband of his affectionate wife. Those who were once the richest among us are reduced to the necessity of begging their bread, while others still remain weltering in their own blood, and deprived of all the comforts of life. And as to the churches in S. Martino and other places, who, on all former occasions, have been a sanctuary to the persecuted, they have themselves now been summoned to quit their dwellings, and every soul of them to depart, and that instantaneously and without respite, under pain of being put to death. Nor is there any mercy to be expected by any of them who are found within the dominions of his royal highness.

"To conclude, our beautiful and flourishing churches are utterly lost, and that without remedy, unless our God work miracles for us. Their time is come, and our measure is full! O, have pity upon the desolations of Jerusalem, and be grieved for the affliction of Joseph. Show forth your compassions, and let your bowels yearn in behalf of so many thousands of poor souls, who are reduced to a morsel of bread, for following the Lamb whithersoever he goeth. We recommend our pastors, with their scattered and dispersed flocks, to your fervent Christian prayers, and rest in haste.

"April, 27th 1655."   "Your brethren in the Lord.

These painful recitals convey but an imperfect idea of the cruelties inflicted upon the Waldenses, by the enemies of pure Gospel.

"They cast some," says Claude, "into large fires, and took them out when they were half roasted. They hanged others with ropes under their arms, and plunged them several times into wells, till they promised to renounce their religion. They tied them like criminals on the rack, and by means of a funnel, poured wine into their mouths, till, being intoxicated, they declared that they consented to turn Catholics. Some they cut and slashed with pen-knives; others they took up by the nose with red-hot tongs, and led them up and down the rooms till they promised to turn Catholics."

Yet true were the lines of Luther, with reference to that noble band of martyrs, in different countries and times:

> "Flung to the heedless winds,
>   Or on the waters cast,
> Their ashes shall be watched,
>   And gathered at the last:
> And from that scattered dust,
>   Around us and abroad,
> Shall spring a plenteous seed
>   Of witnesses for God."

From what has been already said, it is sufficiently obvious, that during the long period of the earlier Christian centuries, religious liberty was nowhere enjoyed. There was not a place upon the face of the earth, where men were wholly free to worship God according to their own individual convictions of duty.

III.

THE REFORMERS OPPOSED TO SOUL-LIBERTY.

And now let it be particularly observed, that the Reformation did not correct the prevailing opinion as to State support, and State interference in matters of religion. The Reformers, so called, without exception, noble men as they were, held firmly this erroneous view.

Says a learned antiquarian writer, "There is not a confession of faith nor a creed framed by any of the Reformers, which does not give to the magistrate coercive power in religion, and almost every one, at the same time, curses the resisting Baptists."

Luther says, of false teachers: "I am averse to the shedding of blood, 'tis sufficient they should be banished or put under restraint as madmen."

Calvin, on the passage, (Luke xiv. 9,) "Compel them to come in," (that is; by the power of motive,) says, "I do not disapprove of the use which Augustine frequently made of this passage against the Donatist, to prove that godly princes may lawfully issue edicts for *compelling* obstinate and rebellious persons to worship the true God, and to maintain the unity of the faith."

Zwingle bitterly persecuted the Baptists; and the name of the gentle Melancthon is associated with the declared sentiment of the diet of Hamburg, that "the Anabaptists may and ought to be restrained by the sword."

In 1530 the magistrates of Zurich published a solemn edict, to prevent the spread of Baptist sentiments; making it *punishable with death* to baptize an individual who had been sprinkled in infancy.

The learned Cranmer could wring from the tender youth of the reluctant Edward, a warrant for the death of those who differed in faith; a warrant signed in tears, and coupled with a clause like Pilate's.

In answer to one of those pleas for Soul-Liberty put forth by the Baptists in Great Britain, the great Scottish Reformer, John Knox, says, with special reference to one denouncing persecution: "I will not now so much labor to confute with my pen, as my full purpose is to lay the same to thy charge, if I shall apprehend thee in any commonwealth where justice against blasphemers may be ministered as God's word requireth." And nearly a century later, the general assembly of the Presbyterian Church, in Scotland, forbade *all printers in the kingdom* from printing or reprinting *any* confession of faith, or protestations, or reasons, *pro or contra,* without warrant."

It is safe to affirm, that during the times now under review, the Baptists were the *only* avowed and consistent advocates of religious freedom. It is true that Jeremy Taylor, an Episcopalian, put forth a plea for toleration in religion. But this plea of his, for the "Liberty of Prophesying," did not take the broad ground assumed by the Baptists. It has been justly said, with reference to it:

One essential principle runs through the writings of Jeremy Taylor and the Dutch Arminians, whose mode of argument he adopted. It is the plea for latitude of interpretation of the State religion, and not for absolute freedom. Their whole argument is founded on the assumption that it is impossible to ascertain from the Scriptures an exact and definite system of belief; hence those sects that do not vary very widely from the State religion ought to be tolerated. Grotius and Episcopius pleaded for the *toleration* of Arminianism by the Calvinists, who were in the majority. Jeremy Taylor pleaded for toleration of Episcopacy by the Presbyterians when they had the power. When Jeremy Taylor became a bishop, he does not seem to have been very faithful even to his own partial view of religious liberty. To the Baptists, therefore, belongs the honor of being the *first* to *promulgate, defend* and *practice* the doctrine of *full and unconditional* freedom of religious belief and worship.

And the noble part they performed in this matter, we shall now begin more fully to see.

At a very early day the Baptists published their "Confessions of Faith," to show precisely what they did believe. And it is interesting to see how nobly they uttered their sentiments touching Soul-Liberty. Among those that have come down to us, is one made in 1611, the same year of the issue of our present English version of the Scriptures: and it was fitting that the issue of these two publications should be contemporaneous events.

Their declarations of principles, on this point, are as one solitary voice crying out in the midst of surrounding darkness. "We believe," say they, "that the magistrate is not to meddle with religion, nor compel men to this or that form of religion, because *Christ is the King and Lawgiver of the Church and of the conscience.*"

In the year 1615 we again hear the Baptists speaking in a published volume after this sort, (against the universally prevailing opinion,) "that no man ought to be persecuted for his religion, so he testify his allegiance by the oath appointed by law." And again: "The power and the authority of the king is earthly, and God hath commanded me to submit to all ordinances of man; and, therefore, I have faith to submit to what ordinances soever the king commands, if it be a human ordinance and *not against the manifest word of God.* Let him require what he will, I must of conscience obey him, with my body, goods, and all that I have."

"But my soul, wherewith I am to worship God, *that* belongeth to *another King,* whose kingdom is not of this world; whose people must come *willingly:* whose weapons are not carnal, but spiritual. If I do take any authority from the king's majesty, let me be judged worthy my desert; but if I defend the authority of Christ Jesus over men's souls, which *appertaineth to no mortal man whatsoever,* then know you, that whosoever would rob him of the honor which is not of this world, he will tread them under foot."

"Earthly authority belongeth to earthly kings, but *spiritual authority* belongeth to that one spiritual King, who is KING OF KINGS."

It is surprising that even Mr. John Robinson, "the father" of the band of exiles for their religion, then in Holland, and afterwards in America, actually put himself in opposition to the published views of the Baptists, in their Confession of Faith, though himself an exile for conscience sake: which is a fair index to the sentiment of that day on this subject. From his retreat in Holland, he published an attack upon the principles of the Baptists, especially objecting to their views of the duty of the magistrate. "I answer," says he, "that this proves that he (the magistrate) may alter, devise, or establish nothing in religion, *otherwise than Christ hath appointed;* but proves not, that he may not use his *lawful power lawfully* for the furtherance of Christ's kingdom and laws. The prophet Isaiah, speaking of the Church of Christ, foretells that kings shall be her nursing fathers, and queens her nursing mothers; which, if they meddle not with her, how can they be? And where these men make this, the magistrates only work, 'that justice and civility may be preserved amongst men.' The Apostle teaches another end, which is, that we may lead a peaceable life under them, in all godliness. It is true that they have no power *against* the laws, doctrine, and religion of Christ; but *for* the same, if their power be of God, they may use it lawfully, *and against the contrary.*"

The same year of the publication of the Confession of Faith now in question, Mr. Wightman, a Baptist was burned in Smithfield. To show still further the sentiment of the time, it may be observed, that when, in 1644, after his return from America, Roger Williams published, in England, his *"Bloody Tenet"*—against persecution for conscience sake — which was dedicated to the two Houses of Parliament, Dr. Lazarus Seaman, in a sermon before Parliament, denounced the work by name. He quotes from the work, and then adds: "Solomon had many wives, seven hundred; let us not have so many religions. Observe the gradation; first connivance, then open toleration, and here with all apostacy." Newcomen, another man of influence, had, but a fortnight before, in his sermon before the same august assembly, denounced the same volume by name. He spoke of the liberty of conscience as an opinion most destructive to the souls of men and to the commonwealth. "I hope," he says, "by your leave, that Parliament will declare that *this must not be.*" The names of Lightfoot and Baxter were also publicly annexed to similar declarations.

Dr. Owen in an essay appended to a sermon preached before Parliament in 1646, after defining a *toleration* as a permission "that every one may be let alone in doing, speaking, acting, how, what, where or when he pleaseth, in all such things as concerneth the worship of God, articles of belief, or generally any thing commanded in religion, and in the mean time the parties at variance, and litigant about differences, freely to revile, reject and despise one another," — that is, opinion left unchecked except by free discussion, declares "that such a toleration would prove *exceeding pernicious* to all sorts of men." These sentiments prevailed in the Westminster Assembly of Divines, and accordingly the Confession of Faith contained an explicit assertion of the duty of the civil magistrate to *suppress heresy.* The doctrine of the assembly is still prevalent, to some extent, in Scotland.

Mr. Hetherington, the author of the history of the Westminster Assembly, thus gravely argues: "Who will say
that... because it is wrong to suppress truth, therefore
it is wrong to suppress crime or discountenance
error" — thus assuming that the magistrate has authority to decide the truth or error of religious opinions.

The Independents are commonly held to have gone
further, and to have adopted the principles of religious
liberty. But it has been justly remarked, that though
some individuals among them may have held just sentiments in *speculation*, they agreed as a body with the
Presbyterian establishment in England. Then they
made common cause with "the sectaries," and seemed to
come nearer to the truth of Soul-Liberty. One of their
writers says, "Princes may and ought, within their
dominions, to abolish all false worship, all false minis-
tries, whatsoever, and to establish the true worship and
ministry appointed by God in his Word; commanding
and compelling their subjects to come unto, and practice
no other but this."

Even the great Lord Bacon applies the term "furies"
to the Anabaptists; and speaks of the "temporal sword"
as an instrument that should be drawn with *great cir-
cumspection in cases of religion."*

And now let the reader observe, that all through
these later times, (that is, the times succeeding the Reformation), as well as in the previous centuries, the Baptists were *enduring* as well as *protesting*. With the sufferings of many of them in England, most are familiar. In
Wales, their sufferings were scarcely less severe. Even
so recently as two hundred years ago, the Baptists in

Wales were prohibited from holding their associations and other public meetings. For twenty-eight years, about this time particularly, they suffered much persecution. Scores of them lost all their property. Mothers and little children suffered the greatest indignities. Whole families were dragged from their homes at midnight, and their houses were burned to the ground. Some were tied to wild horses, while others were dragged for miles in chains. Many were taken in the night from their beds, to the sea-shore, when the tide was at its ebb, so as to be carried away when at its flow. Very many were thrown into prison without trial. Mr. Vavasor Powell spent nearly eleven years in prison, where he died October 27, 1670. Mr. Henry Williams was incarcerated for nine years. When he was taken, the mob murdered his aged father, and burned his house; and it was with great difficulty that his own life and the lives of his children were saved.

All this these praying and devoted people endured, simply because of their religious principles and practices as Baptists.

From this time forth, however, the battle for Soul-Liberty in Great Britain waxed fiercer and wider. John Bunyan and John Milton, (both Baptists,) and scores of others, enlisted as its bold champions; and by slow degrees victories were gained, the ultimate results of which will yet be the complete disenthralment of all Europe from every kind of bondage to the civil power, in the concerns of the soul.

IV.

THE PURITANS AND SOUL-LIBERTY.

Let us now cross the Atlantic, and come to the new settlements in New England. Persecuted for their relig-ion abroad, the Pilgrims and Puritans have sought here an asylum. But, strange to say, the old error of com-pulsion and State interference in matters of religion is not abjured; but, on the contrary, adopted and incor-porated in the very *basis* of the community.* Their idea is, to have a *theocracy*, a God-government, a *State*, which at the same time shall be a *church*, or made up on-ly of church-members. Take these facts in illustration.

In May of 1631, the general court of Massachusetts enacted the following law: "To the end the body of the Commons may be preserved of honest and good men, it is ordered and agreed that, for the time to come, no man be admitted to the freedom of this body politic, but such as are members of *some of the churches* within the limits of the same."†

* It is but justice to say, that the *Pilgrims* of the Plymouth Colony were more liberal in their enactments than the *Puritans* of the Massachusetts Colony.

† Backus History.

Thus a theocracy, or religious aristocracy, was established. Religious opinion and church-membership were made the test of a man's qualifications as a voter or office-holder. In founding the New Haven Colony, it was agreed that, "Free burgesses shall be chosen out of *church members:* they that are in the foundation work of church-fellowship, being actually free burgesses; and to choose to themselves out of the like estate of church-fellowship, and the power of choosing magistrates, etc., and the business of like nature, are to be transacted by these free burgesses."

Mr. Felt, in his "Annals of Salem," says that in 1644, "the bond of Union between Church and State had existed for more than thirty years."

"Church and State," in Massachusetts, says President Quincy, "were very curiously and efficiently interwoven with each other." Judge Story says, speaking of the colonial times: "The arm of the civil government was constantly employed in support of the denunciations of the Church; and without its *form*, the *inquisition* existed, *in substance*, with a full share of its terrors and its violence."

The now flourishing city of Newark, N.J., was founded by settlers from New England, and they carried out the same State-Church policy. This is seen in the first of several provisions which they adopted, as the basis of the civil compact, in October 30th, 1666. The provision was as follows: "That none shall be admitted freemen or free burgesses within our town upon Passaic River, in the Province of New Jersey, but such planters as are men of some or other of the Congregational Churches;

nor shall any but such be chosen to magistracy, etc., — nor shall any but church-members have any vote in any such elections."

We are careful thus to verify these statements, from the frequent attempts, in our times, to give a milder complexion to the doings of the planters of New England, than they will bear; and the disposition to cover up plain facts of history, by fulsome and indiscriminate eulogies. We would not detract from the real virtues of the Puritan character. That man is an object of pity whose admiration is not excited as he contemplates it. But the Pilgrims and Puritans were not demi-gods, as some would make them. They held opinions common to their day. Of true religious freedom they had no idea. If they advocated the rights of conscience, it was that *they* might not be oppressed. They came here to worship God, themselves, unmolested; but they had not the remotest idea of establishing liberty of conscience for any *except those of their own way of thinking.* They would not even *tolerate* those of an opposite faith, much less concede this liberty to differ as their *right.*

They established Congregationalism *by law*, thus making the Baptists and Quakers rebel, and then punished them, by the civil arm, after the clergy had decided on their heresy.*

* A living humorous poet has pretty justly hit the case in the following lines:

"I love the Puritan; and from my youth,
  Was taught to admire his valor and his truth.
  The veriest caviller must acknowledge still
  His honest purpose, and his manly will.
  I own I reverence that peculiar race

To place beyond all question the truth of these remarks, we cite the following additional particulars: In 1636, it was enacted, that "if any Christian shall openly condemn the baptizing of infants, or shall purposely depart the congregation at the administration of that ordinance ... continuing obstinate therein, he shall be

Who valued steeples less than Christian grace:
Preferred a hut where frost and freedom reigned,
To sumptuous halls at freedom's cost obtained,
And proudly scorning all that royal knaves
For bartered conscience sold to cringing slaves,
Gave up their homes for rights respected more
Than all the allurements of their native shore,
In stranger lands their tattered flag unfurled,
And taught this doctrine to a startled world:—
'Mitres and thrones are man-created things,
We own no master but the King of kings.'
'Tis little marvel that their honored name,
Bears, as it must, some macula of shame;
'Tis only pity that they e'er forgot,
The golden lessons their experience taught;
Thought 'Toleration' due to 'saints' alone,
And 'Rights of Conscience' only meant *their own:*
Enforcing laws concocted to their need,
On all non-jurors to the *ruling creed,*
Till Baptists groaned beneath their iron heel,
And Quakers quaked with unaccustomed zeal!
And when I hear, as oft the listener may,
In song and sermon on a festal day,
Their virtues lauded to the wondering skies,
As none were e'er so great, or good, or wise,
I straight bethink me of the Irish wit,
(A people famed for many a ready hit,)
Who, sitting once, and rather ill at ease,
To hear, in prose, such huge hyperboles,
Gave a toast, to chide the fulsome tone,
'Old Plymouth Rock,—the Yankee Blarney Stone!"†

†Mr. Saxe, before Boston Mercantile Library Association.

sentenced to be banished."

In 1644, as Winthrop informs us, "Anabaptistry increased, which occasioned the magistrates, at the last Court, to draw an order for banishing such as continued obstinate."

In 1649, a law was passed, reaffirming the old soul-tyranny, and still making it an offence, to be punished by banishment, to oppose infant baptism. Observe, also, the character of the following extracts from standard authorities:

"It is ordered that no person, being a member of any church, which shall hereafter be gathered without the approbation of the magistrates and the greater part of said churches, shall be admitted to the freedom of this commonwealth." (Mass. Laws, 1636.) "Whoever reproached a magistrate or a minister, or circulated, or did not surrender an unorthodox book, must pay five pounds, or ten pounds, according to the malignity of his crime. Women, for a like offence, were to have a 'cleft-stick' put upon their tongues." (Felt's Salem.)

"The Court having asked advice of the masters about the case of Roger Williams, they replied, in substance, that he deserved to be banished from the colony for maintaining the doctrine 'that a civil magistrate might not intermeddle even to stop a church from apostacy and heresy." (Gammell's Life of R. Williams.) "Toleration was preached against as a sin in rulers, which would bring down the judgments of heaven upon the land." (Hutchinson.) "I believe that Antichrist hath not, at this day, a more probable way to advance his kingdom of darkness than by a toleration of all religions and persuasions." (Increase Mather, Election Sermon, 1677.)

"If any church, one or more, shall grow schismatical, rending itself from the communion of other churches, or shall walk incorrigibly or obstinately in any corrupt way of their own, contrary to the rule of the Word, in such case *the magistrate is to put forth his coercive power as the matter shall require.*" (Cambridge and Saybrook Platform.)

When Cromwell proposed toleration in England, a Massachusetts Synod protested against it as licentious. Norton, of Ipswich, in a publication against it, expressed a censure even of toleration in Holland, where so many oppressed Puritans had found refuge. "I lived," he says, "in a city where a Papist preached in one church, a Lutheran in another, a Calvinist in a third; a Lutheran one part of the day, and a Calvinist the other, in the same pulpit. The religion of that place was but motley and meagre, and their affections leopard-like."

Says the great John Cotton: "It was toleration that made the world anti-Christian, and the Church never took hurt by the punishment of heretics." Ward, the author of the "Simple Cobbler of Agawam," says: "To authorize an untruth, by a toleration of State, is to build a sconce against the walls of heaven, to batter God out of His chair."

In 1672, Shepherd preached his "Eye-Salve" Election Sermon, in which he ascribes toleration to the devil. "'Tis Satan's policy," says he, "to plead for an indefinite and boundless toleration." This same year the General Court revised and reprinted the laws banishing Baptists from the colony. The year following, 1673,

President Oakes, of Harvard College, preached the Election Sermon. "I look upon toleration," said he, "as the first-born of all abominations." In the election sermon of 1676, William Hubbard said: "If he was not mistaken who said, 'It is morally impossible to rivet the Christian religion into the body of a nation without infant baptism,' by proportion it will necessarily follow, that the neglect, or disuse thereof, will directly tend to root it out."

Hubbard, the historian, says that synods and messengers will not keep ecclesiastical peace, "unless they be a little *acuated* by the civil authority." (Actuated meant *sharpened*, — and, as some one remarked, the word was much to the *point!*)

The sentiment of the time was well embodied in some lines found in the pocket of Governor Dudley, after his death in 1650:

"Let men of God, in *Courts* and *Churches*, watch
O'er such as do a TOLERATION hatch:
Lest that ill egg bring forth a cockatrice,
To poison all with heresy and vice."

V.

PERSECUTION OF NEW ENGLAND BAPTISTS.

Such was the state of things in New England, as established by law. And by the influence of Baptists, mainly, was the glorious change, which we now witness, *effected.*

But it was not effected without vast effort, and the endurance of hardship, and loss, and suffering. The mind of the reader turns at once to Roger Williams; a man, for whom no one would claim perfection, but a man of great learning and undoubted piety, concerning whom Southey remarks: "He began the first civil government on the earth which gave equal liberty of conscience;" and of whom Bancroft says, (without sufficient credit to other Baptists, before Williams, *in Europe*,) he was "the first in modern Christendom to assert, in its plenitude, the doctrine of Liberty of Conscience."*

With the career of Williams most are familiar. He

---

* Bancroft proceeds to say of Williams, as the advocate of religious freedom: "In its defence he was the harbinger of Milton, and the precursor and the superior of Jeremy Taylor. For Taylor limited his toleration to a few Christian sects; the philanthropy of Williams compassed the earth." Vol. I., page 376.

arrived in Massachusetts in 1631, and soon began to make known his peculiar sentiments. He would hold no communion with intolerance; for, said he, "the doctrine of persecution for cause of conscience is most evidently and lamentably contrary to the doctrine of Jesus Christ."

"No one should be bound to worship, or maintain a worship, against his own consent." And when his antagonists exclaimed, "Is not the laborer worthy of his hire?" "Yes," replied Williams, *"from them that hire him."*

The advocacy of such sentiments was not to be allowed. He must be banished. He *was* banished; setting out from home in January, 1636.

"For *fourteen weeks*," he says, "I was sorely tossed in a bitter season, not knowing what bread or bed did mean, often in a stormy night, I had neither fire nor food, and no house but a hollow tree."

His wife and two children, the youngest less than three months old, were left behind. By a mortgage on his property at Salem he had raised money to supply his wants. He then plunged into the untrodden wilds; being "denied the common air to breath in, and a civil cohabitation upon the same common earth; yea, and also without mercy and human compassion, exposed to winter in a howling wilderness." After fourteen weeks exposure to frost and snow, he arrived at Seekonk,* on the east bank of the Pawtucket river. Here he began to build and plant. In the following expressive lines he seems to refer to the kind support afforded him by

* Now called *Rehoboth.*

the *Indians:* —

> "God's providence is rich to his,
> Let none distrustful be;
> In wilderness, in great distress,
> These ravens have fed me."

Their hospitality he requited throughout his long life, by acts of benevolence, and by unceasing efforts to benefit and befriend them. He taught them Christianity; and was the first of the American pilgrims to convey to these savage tribes the message of salvation. Before his crops were ripe for harvest, however, he received intimation from the governor of Plymouth, that he had, "fallen into the edge of their bounds," and as they were loath to offend the people of the Bay, he was requested to move beyond their jurisdiction.

With five companions he embarked in his canoe, descending the river, until, arriving at a little cove on the opposite side, they were hailed by the Indians with the cry of *"what cheer?"* Cheered with this friendly salutation, they went ashore. Again embarking, they reached a spot at the mouth of the Mohassuck river, where they landed, near to a spring, — remaining to this day as an emblem of those vital blessings which flow to society from true liberty. That spot is "holy ground," where sprung up the first civil polity in the world permitting freedom to the human soul in things of God. There Roger Williams founded a town, which in gratitide to God, he called Providence.*

It was here that he gave a formal expression to his views on baptism, by being buried with Christ in like-

* See, Struggles and Triumphs of Religious Liberty, p. 235, etc.

ness of his death. As none of the colony had been immersed, a Mr. Holman was selected to baptize Mr. Williams; who then baptized Mr. Holman and ten others: and thus was formed the first Baptist Church in America. Here he established a commonwealth, where, to use his own words, "the will of the majority should govern the State, yet, *only in civil things*. God alone is the *ruler of the conscience*." And again he says of this home of freedom, in words that make the heart burn at their perusal: "All men may here walk as their consciences persuade them, every one in the name of his God. And let the lambs of the Most High walk in this colony without molestation, in the name of Jehovah, their God, for ever and ever."†

† Archbishop Hughes has asserted that the Catholics of Maryland have borne away the prize from Roger Williams and Rhode Island; alleging that they there established religious freedom earlier than it was established in Rhode Island. But in the first place, the civil code of Maryland, was instituted *two years later than* that of Rhode Island — the latter in 1647; the former in 1649. In the next place, the law in Maryland, *did not establish* ENTIRE *religious* freedom, at all. The act is 16 and 17 Cecilius, Lord Baltimore. (See laws of Maryland at large, by T. Bacon, A.D. 1765.) Here are some of its provisions.

Blasphemy against God, denying our Saviour Jesus Christ to be the Son of God, or denying the Holy Trinity, or the Godhead of any of the three persons, etc., was to be punished with death and confiscation of lands and goods to the Lord Proprietory. Persons using any reproachful words or speeches concerning "the *Blessed Virgin Mary*, Mother of our Saviour, or the Holy Apostles or Evangelists, or any of them," for the offence to forfeit £15, sterling to the Lord Proprietory; or in default of payment, to be *publicly whipped*, and *imprisoned* at the pleasure of his Lordship, or his Lieut. General. For the second offence to forfeit £10, sterling, and for the third to forfeit land and goods, and be for

It is also worthy of note, that, not content with banishment alone, the authorities of Massachusetts passed a decree in 1638, that no inhabitant of Providence should even come into their jurisdiction, for any purpose whatever, (unless he was willing to admit the right of the magistrates, to exercise power in the church,) under the severest penalties.

Thus much for this apostle of religious liberty. But Roger Williams is by no means alone in the glory of having suffered for the truth's sake, in those times of intolerance. Hundreds and thousands shared with him this honor.

Among the few who must be referred to, stands Obediah Holmes, who was whipped in 1651. He denied the scripturalness of infant baptism, and would immerse instead of sprinkle. He moreover boldly proclaimed sentiments of Soul-Liberty. It was not to be endured. The executioner must chastise him. The scene occurred in Boston. His clothes were stripped from him. He was tied to the public whipping-post. The cruel thongs of the three-corded whip dashed the gore from the quivering flesh, as it was plied with all the strength of the brutal officer. God, however, was with him; for he says: "As the strokes fell upon me, I had such a spiritual manifestation of God's presence as I never had before, and the outward pain was so removed from me that I well could

ever *banished out of the Province.*

These are some of the provisions of this famous enactment, which only secures to *Catholics* and *Trinitarians* the right of worship, consigning all others to fines, imprisonment, scourging and banishment. What a contrast between this act and the law of Rhode Island, whose liberal enactments are given above!

bear it; yea, I felt it not; although it was grievous, as the spectators said, the man striking with all his strength, spitting in his hand three times, with a three-corded whip, giving me therewith thirty strokes." He told the magistrates when untied from the post: "you have struck me with roses, and although the Lord hath made it easy to me, I pray God, it may not be laid to your charge." John Hazel and John Spur came and shook hands with him, smiling, and saying, "Blessed be God!" for which they were arrested on the spot, fined forty shillings, and imprisoned.

Holmes was so bruised and wounded that for weeks he could rest only on his hands and knees; and yet in this state he left home and made his way through the forest-wilderness to Providence, to escape a second arrest by the constable. He returned, however, afterwards, to Newport, where he lived to a good old age, and in 1790, his descendants were reckoned at not less than five hundred persons.*

To show the tone of public opinion at this time, it may be stated that John Cotton, (who wrote a reply to Williams' book against persecution in religion—"The Bloody Tenet"—which reply, Cotton styled, *The bloody tenet washed and made white in the blood of the Lamb!*") actually justified and defended the whipping of this good minister, Obediah Holmes; nor was there, then, in all New England, a solitary minister publicly to dissent from these views of John Cotton, or say a word for the liberty of conscience, with the exception of the Baptists.

* Hildreth Vol I.

A single passage from a letter of Mr. Cotton to a friend in England, in which he apologizes for this infliction of thirty lashes, with a three-corded whip, on Obediah Holmes, will reveal the spirit of those who were leaders in this persecution. "The offense," says he, "was a manifest contestation against the order and government of our churches, established, we know, by God's law, and as he, Holmes, knows, by the laws of the country. If the worship be lawful in itself, the magistrate, compelling to it, compelleth not to sin, but the sin is in his will, that needs to be compelled to a Christian duty."

There were no lengths to which one could not justify himself in proceeding, who could thus apply to his soul the unction of conscious loyalty to God. The Baptists were opposing a church government, which Cotton did not merely think or believe, but which he *knew* accorded with the law of God. Of course, he could see him punished with a zest!

We refer to a few other examples of suffering from intolerance: From 1727 to 1733, twenty-eight Baptists were imprisoned at Bristol, by the constables at Rehoboth, for ministerial taxes. About the middle of the same century, a Baptist minister — Hezekiah Smith — went to Haverhill to preach, and when it was known to what denomination he belonged, his presence could not be endured; and the "Selectmen" of the town commissioned an officer to warn him out of the place. The officer who was sent to read the notice, was so awed by Mr. Smith's dignified presence, that he could not read it; but tremblingly stammered out: "I — I — warn you — off — God's earth!" The good man, however, remained, and lived down opposition, and accomplished a great work in the Master's cause.

About this time, according to Winthrop, in his journal, a poor man by the name of Painter, refused to bring his child to be sprinkled, thinking it to be wrong. For this he was barbarously flogged like a common felon. Winthrop says: *"He was very poor; so as no other but corporal punishment could be fastened upon him, he was ordered to be whipped."*

It is on record that a pastor of a Baptist church in Wallingford, Conn., (established in 1739,) by the name of John Merriam, was imprisoned, and his feet made fast in the stocks, for no other crime than preaching the doctrines of the Bible as held by Baptists. It is also on record that Rev. Philemon Robins, pastor of the Congregational Church in Bradford, in the year 1742, preached to this Baptist Church in Wallingford, by request of their pastor. For doing this he was complained of to the Consociation of Congregational Churches in New Haven county. No acknowledgment from him would satisfy the Consociation, short of a confession that he had violated the law of God in preaching to an unlawful society. But such a confession he could not be induced to make. He was therefore deposed from the ministry, and excluded from the fellowship of the churches. The Church in Bradford, however, sustained their pastor in his course.

For a public exhortation at Lynn, in 1651, at the house of a friend, on Sunday morning, Mr. Clarke, a Baptist minister, was arrested, carried by force, and made to hear a Pedo-Baptist minister, then the next day sent to Boston, and sentenced to pay 20 pounds, or be whipped.

In a sermon just before the trial, John Cotton declared that to deny infant baptism was to overthrow all, and was therefore soul-murder, and a capital offence; and so the Governor (Endicott) maintained in passing the sentence against Mr. Clarke.*

In 1654, Dunster, the learned President of Harvard College, was indicted, tried, and fined for the expression of Baptist opinions, and was obliged to resign his office. Chauncey, his successor, who held to immersion, though not denying infant baptism, was allowed to hold office by keeping his opinions to himself.†

In 1657, a law was enacted, declaring that every male Quaker was to have one ear cut off on the first conviction, and the other ear on the second; and both males and females, on a third conviction, were to have their tongues bored through with a red-hot iron.

Several of this sect were afterwards executed.

At Rehoboth,‡ in Plymouth, in the year 1663, a number of the Baptists separated themselves from the church there established, and for several years maintained themselves, undisturbed, as a separate society. But in 1667, they were summoned before the General Court, and fined for establishing public meetings to "the disturbance of the peace of the place." They were required to discontinue these meetings within one month's time, as their continuance in Rehoboth, being very prejudicial to the peace of the Church and the town, could not be allowed. "Yet," (thus concludes

* Hildreth I., 380.
† Hildreth, p. 392.
‡ The place was also called Seawek.

this act of the General Court of Plymouth,) "in case they shall remove their meeting into some other place, where they may not prejudice any other church, and shall give us reasonable satisfaction respecting their principles, we know not but that they may be permitted by this government to do so." As the result of this permission these Baptists founded a church in Swansea, on the borders of the colony of Rhode Island, and lived without farther molestation by the government, under the ministry of Mr. Miles, who had fled from Swansea, in Wales, after the Uniformity Act there of 1662.

In 1665, the leading members of the Baptist Church, at Charlestown, Mass., were brought before the Court, and sentenced to be disfranchised, and, upon conviction, to be committed to prison, simply because they maintained public religious worship on Sunday.

One of the spectators having remarked openly: "The Court has not to do in matters of religion;" he was arrested, and it was only upon his confession that he saw his fault, and was sorry for it, that he was dismissed with an admonition from the Governor.

In the year 1768, on a very cold night in winter, about nine or ten o'clock in the evening, Mrs. Martha Kimball, of Bradford, was taken prisoner, and carried by the collector in the town where she lived, from her family, consisting of three small children, in order to be put to jail. It being a severe cold night, she concluded, by advice, while she was detained in a tavern on the way to jail, to pay the sum for which she was made a prisoner, it being for the *ministerial rate*. The reason why she refused paying it before, was, because she was a Baptist, and belonged to the Baptist Society.

She then walked home (two miles) through the snow and cold in the dead of night. The same year, three hundred and ninety-eight acres of land, valued at three hundred and sixty-three pounds sterling, were taken, by law, from certain Baptists in Ashfield, and sold towards meeting the expenses of the Established Church there. One poor man's dwelling house, and the burying-ground of the Baptists, were also sold for church rates.

A Baptist Church was constituted in Chelmsford in October, 1771. In the following March, the town voted to raise a sum of money to pay the town charges, and to support their minister. The taxes were made during the same month, and were assessed upon the Baptists as well as others. The money was, moreover, ordered to be immediately collected. Although the Baptists had carried in certificates according to law, the collector said they were a praying people, and he would put them all into jail together, when they would have nothing else to do *but* pray.

This he began to do on the 6th of January, 1773. When he came to the house of Mr. Nathan Crosby, with a large number of assistants, a woman, who lived in another part of the house, told him that Mr. Crosby was sick, and not able to go to prison. But one of the company declared that, if he were sick, and in bed, and if they took him out, and he died in their hands, nobody would hurt them.

Mr. Crosby entreated the collector to let him remain till he should be better, which the latter seemed inclined to do.

But one of the assistants, who had given the collector

a dollar to induce him to carry Crosby to jail that very day, insisted that it should be done. The warrant was then served, and he was ordered to get ready. The collector, however, allowed him to ride with himself, on his horse; but as he left his wife and children in tears, some of the company told them he would be put in a room without fire, where he would freeze to death. The collector next took Gershom Proctor, who was about eighty-two years of age; then his son Henry Proctor, both of whom had carried in certificates. Henry left a wife and seven small children, with no one to assist them but a young man who was then sick. They were all committed to Concord jail.

Eighteen men in Warwick, shortly after this, were imprisoned from failure to pay the church rates, in the Northampton jail, forty miles from home in the extremity of winter.*

In 1680, the doors of the first Baptist Church, Boston were nailed up by the Marshal, and a notice posted thereon, reading thus:

"All persons are to take notice that by order of court, the doors of this house are shut, and that they are inhibited to hold any meetings therein, or to open the doors thereof, without license from the authorities, till the court take further order, as they will answer the contrary at their peril.

"A true copy from the record.

"EDWARD RAWSON, Sec'y."

* See Life and Times of Backhus, 182.

On the return of the Sabbath the little despised band, were compelled to worship God under a temporary covering in the yard of the meeting-house.

Besides the severe losses and sufferings sustained by the early Baptists of New England for their principles, it is impossible to form any adequate idea of the almost perpetual annoyances which they endured. In some of the fragmentary documents from their hands, which have come down to us, we read of seizures, by law, upon their household utensils, such as, "skillets, kettles, pots, and warming-pans, and pewter, and spinning-wheels," and other items of property, such as "workmen's tools, and oxen, and cows, and swine," which were all sold to pay the expenses of keeping up the "Orthodox" churches.

Without extending, however, these painful recitals, it is sufficient to remark, that the laws to support the clergy of the standing order, and to tax and oppress nonconformists, continued in force long after our national independence was achieved.

It is true that special laws were in some cases passed exempting Baptists and Quakers, upon filing certificates of their belief, from such taxes; but these laws were limited, and had no penalty, and were practically useless. As proof of this, and also as an illustration of the times, the following is copied from the "Minutes of the Philadelphia Association, for the year 1770." It is an extract from letters received from New England at that time, and demonstrates conclusively that the alliance of Church and State in Massachusetts was no less tyrannical and despotic than in the mother country.

"The laws of this province (Massachusetts) were never intended to exempt Baptists from paying towards building and repairing Presbyterian meeting-houses, and making up Presbyterian minister's salaries; for, beside other insufficiencies, they are all limited, both as to extent and duration. The first law extended only five miles around each Baptist meeting-house; those without this circle had no relief, neither had they within, for though it exempted their polls, it left their estates to the mercy of harpies, and their estates went to wreck. The Baptists sought a better law, and with great difficulty and waste of time and money obtained it; but even this was not universal.

"It extended not to any parish *until a Presbyterian meeting-house should be built,* and *a Presbyterian minister settled* there; in consequence of which, the Baptists have never been freed from the first and great expense of their parishes; expenses equal to the current expenses of ten or twelve years. This is the present case of the people of Ashfield, which is a Baptist settlement. There were but five families of other denominations in the place when the Baptist church was constituted; but those five more, have lately built a Presbyterian meeting-house there, and settled an Orthodox minister as they call him, which cost them £200. To pay for both, they laid a tax on the land; and as the Baptists are most numerous, the greater part fell to their share. The Presbyterians in April last demanded their money.

"The Baptists plead poverty, alleging that they had been twice driven from their plantations by the Indians in the last war; that they were but new settlers, and cleared but a few spots of land; and had not been able to build commodious dwelling-houses. Their tyrants would not hear. Then the Baptists plead the ingratitude of such conduct; for they had built a fort there at their own expense, and had maintained it for two years, and so had protected the interior Presbyterians, as well as their neighbors, who now rose up against them; that the Baptists to the westward had raised money to relieve Presbyterians who had, like them, suffered by the Indians; and that it was cruel to take from them what the Indians had left.

"But nothing touched the hearts of these cruel people. Then the Baptists urged the law of the province; but were soon told that the law extended to new parishes till the meeting-house and minister were paid for. Then the Baptists petitioned the General Court. Proceedings were stopped till further orders, and the poor people went home rejoicing — thinking their property safe; but had not all got home before said order came, and it was an order for the Presbyterians to proceed.

"Accordingly in the month of April they fell foul on their estates and left them hardly any but a wilderness. They sold the house and garden of one man, and the young orchards, meadows and cornfields of others; nay, they sold their dead, for they sold their graveyard. The orthodox minister was one of the purchasers."

All this, it must be remembered, was done *by law!* And millions of property in Massachusetts, and Maine, and Connecticut, to-day, are held by a claim no better than that it was taken from Baptists, long ago, for church rates.

In fact, it was not until the year 1834, that the last link connecting Church and State, in Massachusetts, was broken by abolishing the law requiring a general assessment for the support of public worship. One after another, however, the obnoxious enactments were repealed. The influence of the Baptists could not be resisted. Mr. Isaac Backus was especially active. He carried to the Massachusetts Assembly and the Provincial Congress, petitions setting forth the rights of conscience, in a bold and fearless manner. He also published extensively in the same direction. Other Baptist ministers employed their pens with great effect, and every Baptist pulpit in the land protested against oppression for religious views.

The times, too, were big with important events. James II., just now, annuls the charter of the colonies at his will. The Plymouth and Massachusetts colonies, in 1792, are united under one charter; the toleration act in England, had already been passed; and although a century's annoyances are yet to be endured, the friends of Soul-Liberty can not be persecuted with the rigor of former days. What is more important, the Spirit of God is poured out, in the middle of the following century, and Jonathan Edwards, in his masterly writings, delineates with wonderful precision, the churches of the New Testament, and thousands who receive his doctrines carry them to results which he never anticipated, and Baptist churches spring up and multiply in all directions. Every member of these churches is true to the rights of conscience, and by his influence contributes towards the formation of a right public sentiment; the end of all which

is, that there is not now upon all the statute books of
New England, a law abridging the freedom of religious
opinion and practice.

VI.

STRUGGLES FOR SOUL-LIBERTY IN VIRGINIA.

Another grand arena, where the strife of opinion on religious freedom waxed warm, was VIRGINIA — settled before New England; but fighting this battle, nevertheless, *principally* at a late date. Hither let us now turn.

While New England was settled mainly by the Congregationalists and Presbyterians, Virginia was planted by the Church of England, or Episcopalians. As the former incorporated their religious views into the government, to the exclusion of all others, so did the latter theirs. Accordingly we find in the code of Sir Thomas Dale (1611,) this enactment: — "There is not one man, nor woman, in this colony now present, nor hereafter to arrive, but shall give up an account of his, and their faith, and religion, and repair unto the minister, that by his conference with them, he may understand and gather whether heretofore, they have been sufficiently instructed, and catechised in the principles and grounds of religion, etc. In case he refuse, the governor shall cause the offender, for the first time of refusal, to be whipped; for the second time, to be whipped twice, and to acknowledge his fault upon the Sabbath-day, in the congregation; and for the third time, to be whipped every day, until he hath made the same acknowledgement, and asked forgiveness of the same, and shall repair unto the minister to be further instructed as aforesaid."*

In 1623, an act provided that "in every plantation or settlement, there should be a house or room set apart for the worship of God," which worship was commanded and required to be strictly, "in accordance with the constitutions and canons of the Church of England." For these places of worship, ministers were provided by the State, and their salaries paid out of the public treasury by a tax levied upon the people for that purpose.†

To preserve "the purity of doctrine and unity of the Church," it was enacted, during the session of 1643, that "all ministers shall be conformable to the orders and constitution of the Church of England; that no others shall be permitted to *preach or teach*, publicly or privately;" and that "the Governor and Council shall take care that all *nonconformists depart the colony*, with all conveniency."‡ Each person was to attend the parish church of his own parish, or pay fifty pounds of tobacco; and each nonconformist should pay twenty pounds sterling for each month's absence.

Many enactments of this nature, if not, indeed, the *most* of them, looked to the suppression of the Baptists, who, though not permitted to organize into churches, were already here in considerable numbers.

* Laws, etc., Strachey, London, 1612.
† Henning.
‡ Henning's Statutes, Vol. I.

If this were not sufficiently evident from the nature of the case, the following act, in 1661-2, will make it plain: "Whereas many schismatical persons, out of their averseness to the orthodox established religion, or out of the newfangled conceits of their own heretical inventions, *refuse to have their children baptized:* Be it therefore enacted, by the authority aforesaid, that all persons that, in contempt of the divine sacrament of baptism, shall refuse, when they may carry their child, (children) to a lawful minister in that county, to have them baptized, shall be amerced two thousand pounds of tobacco, half to the informer, half to the public."*

And these enactments, with others that followed, were rigidly enforced. Those holding Baptistic views, preachers and laymen, were fined and imprisoned, and otherwise harassed; and as churches were organized, they met with the severest opposition, and the heaviest disabilities.

Even an Episcopalian divine, (Dr. Hawks), in writing the annals of "the Church" in Virginia, is compelled to remark that, "no dissenters in Virginia experienced, for a time, harsher treatment than did the Baptists. They were *beaten and imprisoned; and cruelty taxed its ingenuity to devise new modes of punishment and annoyance.*"

But persecution made them love each other and their principles more warmly; and it also excited the public admiration and sympathy in their behalf. It is of the nature of persecution, to cause those persecuted to grow and flourish. As an old writer has beautifully ex-

* Henning. Vol. II. 164-5.

pressed it—"God's children are like stars, that shine brightest in the darkest night; like torches, that are the better for beating; like grapes, that come not to the proof till they come to the press; like trees, that drive down their roots further, and grasp the earth tighter, by reason of the storm; like vines, that grow the better for bleeding; like the chamomile which spreads the more as you tread upon it."

And so it proved in this case. From a few scores of scattered individuals, the Virginia Baptists have arisen to nearly *one hundred thousand church members.**

The ministers, though imprisoned, continued to preach. It came to be a common remark, that it would do no good to imprison the Baptist preachers—they would keep on preaching from their prison windows. And it was not without the Spirit's power. Rev. Eleazor Clay— a Baptist minister, and a relative and guardian of the statesman, Henry Clay—writes from his residence to Rev. John Williams, "We wish you to come down and baptize those who are now waiting for an opportunity. The Lord is carrying on a glorious work in our county (Chesterfield). The preaching at the prison is not at-

* There are now in the United States about a million of Baptists in *regular church fellowship.* The following Table shows their strength at certain periods, and their numerical progress up to the year 1858.

Year	Churches	Members	Year	Churches	Members
1762	56	8,000	1832	5,320	384,926
1784	471	35,101	1840	7,766	570,758
1790	733	50,970	1851	11,355	838,723
1810-12	2,164	175,138	1857	17,002	1,263,448
1825	3,793	238,100			

tended in vain, for we hope that several are converted, while others are under great distress, and made to cry out, 'What shall we do to be saved?'"

Moreover, these very persecutions enlisted in their behalf some of the noblest spirits of the day. Patrick Henry, particularly, was proud to take their part. Nowhere among his remains is found a more thrilling burst of eloquence, than in his defense of three Baptist ministers, brought to trial in Virginia, in 1775, for preaching. The scene is thus narrated: The indictment brought against them was "for preaching the Gospel of the Son of God," contrary to the statute in that case provided, and, therefore, disturbers of the peace. The clerk was reading the indictment in a slow and formal manner, and he pronounced the crime, with emphasis, *"for preaching the Gospel of the Son of God,"* when a plain-dressed man dismounted from his horse, entered the court-house, and took his seat within the bar. He was known to the Court and lawyers, but a stranger to the mass of spectators who had gathered on the occasion. This was Patrick Henry, who, on hearing of this prosecution, had rode some fifty or sixty miles, from his residence in Hanover county, to volunteer his services in the defence of the prisoners. He listened to the further reading of the indictment with marked attention, the first sentence of which, that had caught his ear, was, *"for preaching the Gospel of the Son of God."*

When the indictment had been read, and the prosecuting attorney had submitted a few remarks, Henry arose, stretched out his hand, and received the paper, and then addressed the court:

"May it please your worships: I think I heard read by the prosecutor as I entered this house, the paper I now hold in my hand. If I have rightly understood, the king's attorney of this colony has framed an indictment for the purpose of arraigning and punishing, by imprisonment, three inoffensive persons before the bar of this court, for a crime of great magnitude—as disturbers of the peace. May it please the court, what did I hear read? Did I hear it distinctly, or was it a mistake of my own? Did I hear an expression, as if a crime, that these men, whom your worships are about to try for a misdemeanor, are charged with—what?" and continuing in a low, solemn, heavy tone, *"for preaching the Gospel of the Son of God."* Pausing, amidst the most profound silence and breathless astonishment of his hearers, he slowly waved the paper three times around his head, then lifting up his hands and eyes to heaven, with extraordinary and impressive energy, he exclaimed: "GREAT GOD!" The exclamation, the action, the burst of feeling from the audience were all over-powering. Mr. Henry resumed:

"May it please your worships: In a day like this, when truth is about to burst her fetters—when mankind are about to be raised to claim their natural and inalienable rights — when the yoke of oppression, which has reached the wilderness of America, and the unnatural alliance of ecclesiastical and civil power, is about to be dissevered—at such a period when liberty—liberty of conscience—is about to awake from her slumberings, and inquire into the reasons of such charges as I find exhibited here to-day in this indictment!"— —Another fearful pause, while the speaker alternately cast his sharp, piercing eyes on the court and the prisoners, and resumed: "If I am not deceived, according to the contents of the paper I now hold in my hand, these men are accused of *'preaching the Gospel of the Son of God.'* — GREAT GOD!"

Another long pause, during which he again waved the indictment around his head, while a deeper impression was made on the auditory. Resuming his speech: "May it please your worships, there are periods in the history of man, when corruption and depravity have so long debased the human character, that man sinks under the weight of the oppressor's hand, and becomes his servile, his abject slave; he licks the hand that smites him; he bows in passive obedience to the mandates of the despot, and in this state of servility, he receives his fetters of perpetual bondage. But, may it please your worship, such a day has passed away!

"From the period when our fathers left the land of their nativity for settlement in these American wilds — for liberty — for civil and religious liberty — for liberty of conscience — to worship their Creator according to their conceptions of heaven's revealed will; from the moment they placed their feet on the American continent, and in the deeply imbedded forests, sought an asylum from persecution and tyranny — from that moment despotism was crushed, her fetters of darkness were broken, and heaven decreed that man should be free -- free to worship God according to the Bible. Were it not for this, in vain have been taken the efforts and sacrifices of the colonists; in vain were all their sufferings and bloodshed to subjugate this new world; if we, their offspring, must still be oppressed and persecuted. But may it please your worships, permit me to inquire once more—for what are these men about to be tried? This paper says, *for preaching the Gospel of the Son of God!'* GREAT GOD! *For preaching the Saviour to Adam's fallen race!'"*

After another pause, in tones of thunder, he inquired, *"What law have they violated?"* Then for the third time, in a slow dignified manner, he lifted up his eyes to heaven, and waved the indictment around his head. The court and the audience were now wrought up to the most intense pitch of excitement. The face of the prosecuting attorney was pale and ghastly, and he appeared unconscious that his whole frame was agitated with alarm; and the Judge, in a tremulous voice, put an end to the scene, now becoming extremely painful, by the authoratative command, *"Sheriff, discharge those men!"*

Another incident, of much the same nature, may be narrated. Among the early Baptist ministers of Virginia, but few were more distinguished than Elder John Weatherford. Wherever he went, vast crowds attended his ministry, and many were the converts that he had the privilege of burying with Christ in Baptism. While on a preaching tour, in the year 1773, he was imprisoned in Chesterfield jail, on the charge of *preaching the Gospel without legal authority.* In the early part of his imprisonment, he was permitted to stand in the door of the jail and preach to the crowd without. This privilege denied him, he then preached through the grates of his prison window. But his enemies were so enraged at his success, that they erected a high wall in front of his window. Crowds still assembled, and as a signal for him to commence his sermon, a handkerchief would be lifted up on a pole above the top of the wall.

And, as one result of his preaching, a number of persons professed conversion, and were baptized, by another minister, by night.

While Mr. Weatherford was thus confined in prison, he heard that, on the other side of James river, resided a distinguished lawyer by the name of Henry, who was the warm friend of the persecuted Baptists. Through the kindness of a friend, poor Weatherford sent to this lawyer five pounds in gold, wrapped up in an old, tattered handkerchief, with the request that he would use his efforts to procure his release. In response to this request Patrick Henry came and succeeded in securing his deliverance, and then returned to him the same old tattered handkerchief, with the five pounds in gold. From that time, until the day of Henry's death, Elder John Weatherford resided (a poor man) in the immediate vicinity of his benefactor, and many were the favors that he continued to receive at his hands.

Patrick Henry never made a public profession of religion. Not a few of his descendants, however, are, at this time, consistent members of Baptist churches.

It will readily be seen, that cases of persecution such as these, instead of hindering, really helped the cause of the Baptists.

And thus, in process of years, they began to be felt as no mean power. To secure religious freedom, was, at that time, the one thing for which they prayed and struggled. In 1774, they appointed, as an association, a day of prayer "in behalf of our *poor blind persecutors,* and *for releasement of our brethren.* "

To secure this soul-freedom, they entered into all the practical questions of the day. They believed that religion should be carried into *every* thing, and should shape and control every force in society, with its silent and pervasive power. They actually appointed for years and years in succession, in their *associational capacity,* delegates, as commissioners to go to the seat of the *State Legislature,* and sometimes to *Congress,* and operate in the making and amending of laws. And mark here, now, the mightly influence which the Baptists exerted on behalf of Soul-Liberty, not only in their own borders, but over the whole land; owing to the *example* of this old state, Virginia, upon those afterwards formed, and the direct contact of their ministers, with the men who laid the basis of our constitutional existence as a people.

Look at this fact. In the year 1775, owing to our difficulties with the mother country, and the obviously approaching crisis of affairs in respect to the American colonies, a general political Convention was assembled in Virginia, to take into consideration the interests of the country. This was the Convention that instructed their delegates in Congress to exert their influence in favor of a declaration of Independence.

The Baptists, who, to a man, were in favor of Independence, (as they felt, in a double sense, the iron oppression,) seized upon this as a favorable moment. They sent a *memorial* to this Convention, touching two things: First, The *civil* freedom of the colonies; and Second, *religious* freedom.

As to the first, they said, in this memorial, that it was their belief that *we ought to make a military resistance to Great Britain;* and that their *ministers* would encourage their young men to enter *the service of their country.* As to the second point, they embodied in that memorial sentiments like the following, which were read, and debated upon, and placed on record; and which must have done much to impregnate the founders of our civil institutions with right views, and stimulate them to right actions.

They said: "We hold, that the mere *toleration* of religion by the civil government is *not sufficient;* that no State religious establishment ought to exist; that all religious denominations ought to stand *upon the same footing;* and that to all, alike, the protection of the government should be extended, securing to them the peaceable enjoyment of their own religious principles and modes of worship.

"We hold it for a fundamental and inalienable truth," they continued, "that the religion of every man must be left to the conviction and conscience of every man. If 'all men, by nature, equally free and independent,' all men are to be considered as entering into society on equal conditons... An established religion implies, either that the civil magistrate is a competent judge of religious truths, or that he may employ religion as an engine of civil policy. The first is an arrogant pretension, falsified by the extravagant opinions of rulers, in all ages, and throughout the world; the second, an unhallowed perversion of the means of salvation."*

Here let it be understood, that these sentiments were, at that time, advocated almost exclusively by the Baptists. The Presbyterians were then a very small body in Virginia; and their testimony was cautious, timid, guarded and *vacillating*. As to the Methodists and Episcopalians, they violently opposed the separation of Church and State. The Baptists were held responsible for the measures looking to this, and they *only;* and so they themselves understood it.

The above memorial was carried to the Convention, which was held at the Capital of the State, by three leading Baptist ministers, who remained there to secure, if possible, their ends.

With three famous men, then at the capital, these Baptist ministers immediately formed an intimate acquaintance, and with them they held long and frequent conversations as to the points involved. And when their names are given, it will be seen, still farther, that these Baptists were working at the foundation of things. They were, THOMAS JEFFERSON, JAMES MADISON, and PATRICK HENRY—the three great moulders and framers of our institutions.

Besides; the first Continental Congress had not been ten days in session, in Philadelphia, when an agent of the Baptists "knocked at the door of the old Carpenters' Hall, to ask that *freedom of conscience* might be given— not to themselves alone, but to *all the dwellers of the land."*

* Semple's Hist., Virg. Bapt. 435.

Over and over again, at all times, and in all possible ways, did the Baptists repeat and urge their views as to Soul-Liberty; and not in vain. By degrees, and through much hostility, they carried their points, until they saw the State Church establishment in Virginia demolished; taxation, by the civil power, for the support of the clergy, even of one's own denomination, done away; the glebes, or church-lands, sold; and, finally, their distinguished views as to Soul-Liberty incorporated into the Constitution of the Federal Union, adopted in 1787, and amended, so as to secure still more perfectly religious freedom, in 1789.

VII.

INDEBTEDNESS OF THE WORLD TO BAPTISTS.

Now, taking into view the powerful influence which Virginia and Virginians exerted over the formation of the government of the younger States, as well as of our National Confederacy; and then re-remembering *how* this prodigious influence of Virginia came to be a *right* influence; and then calling to mind the *other* controlling section of our country—New England—and how IT came, ultimately, to exert a right influence; how apparent is the indebtedness of the people of the United States to the Baptists, for that priceless boon of Religious Freedom in which, to-day, they rejoice! Where had been these our liberties, but for the hard blows which the head of Tyranny received from the staunch old Baptist champions of Freedom for body and spirit? It has been said, with truth, that had "they been silent, the whipping-post and the pillory might still have flourished, and a State Church have extended its despotic sway over all classes of citizens."

Mrs. Heman's has sung of the Pilgrims:

"They have left unstained, what there they found,
FREEDOM to worship GOD."

But it had not been true, that they left "unstained" this freedom, except for the action of the mighty influences here developed. It is certain, beyond question, that the aspect of our institutions had been entirely different, but for the influence of the Baptists.

And not of *our* institutions, only, be it here observed. For the influences here developed, have operated, and are now operating powerfully upon every part of the civilized world. The old hierarchies of England, and of the Continent of Europe, particularly, are being gradually but surely penetrated and undermined by these influences. The German philosopher Gervinus, in a new work, lately published, entitled "An Introduction to the History of the Nineteenth Century," in discussing the doctrines of the Reformation, and their influence upon the world, thus speaks of Roger Williams, and the doctrines first evolved by that illustrious reformer:

"In accordance with these principles, Roger Williams insisted in Massachusetts upon allowing entire freedom of conscience, and upon entire separation of the Church and the State. But he was obliged to flee, and, in 1636, he formed in Rhode Island, a small and new society, in which perfect freedom in matters of faith was allowed, and in which the majority ruled in all civil affairs. Here, in a little State, the fundamental principles of political and ecclesiastical liberty practically prevailed, before they were even taught in any of the schools of philosophy in Europe. At that time people predicted only a short existence for these democratical experiments —universal suffrage, universal eligibility to office, the annual change of rulers, perfect religious freedom—

—the Miltonian doctrine of schisms. But not only have these ideas and these forms of government maintained themselves here, but, precisely from this little State, have they extended themselves throughout the United States. They have conquered the aristocratic tendencies in Carolina and New York, the high-church in Virginia, the theocracy in Massachusetts, and the monarchy in all America. They have given laws to a continent, and, formidable through their moral influence, *they lie at the bottom of all the democratic movements which are now shaking the nations of Europe.*"

If any denomination, therefore, has a HISTORY, and one for which it and the world should be thankful, that denomination is the Baptists. It has ever practiced, and effectually taught, the great truth, that as every man is held directly accountable to GOD for his religious faith and practice, he cannot, of right, be held accountable to any *human* tribunal; but, on the other hand, may claim the heaven-descended and inalienable *right* to be left free from all arrogance, and every form of compulsion, in the affiars of his soul.

And the remark that the Baptists have ever *practised* upon this doctrine, as well as proclaimed it, is worthy of note; for, in this respect, the Baptists stand alone. Other denominations have persecuted. The Romanists have persecuted. The Episcopalians have persecuted. The Presbyterians and Congregationalists have persecuted. The Methodists, as springing from the Church of England, and joining hands to uphold Church and State in Virginia, have persecuted. But, to its praise be it spoken, search the annals of this denomination from the days of John the Baptist until now, and not one line of that history will be found blotted by the record of a deed of persecution! It is sometimes said that this people are il-liberal, bigoted, exclusive; but surely no charge could be more unjust. Their whole history and their uniform bear-ings are proof to the contrary.

We repeat it, then, that the indebtedness of the world, and especially of the people of this country, to the Baptists, is beyond estimate. To blot out every ray of light cast upon the great doctrine of Soul-Liberty by Arnold of Brescia, and Busher, Hubmeyer, and Helwisse, and Milton, and Bunyan of the old world, and by Williams and Backus, and Baldwin, and Leland, and Gano, and Going, and Walker, and Walling, and Knollys, and Stillman, and Clark, and Manning, and their coadjutors in the new, were to turn back, for centuries, the shadow on the dial-plate of time! To withdraw from the temple of our Liberties every stone, either laid by Baptist hands or cemented by Baptist blood, were to mar, beyond repair, its fair proportions, if not to precipitate the fabric into hopeless ruin!

It were easy to show the large indebtedness of this nation to the Baptists for *civil* freedom. They were among the first for advocating and supporting our Revolutionary movements, as Washington himself publicly testified after coming to the Presidency.*

Is it certain, moreover, that William Penn did not owe to his father, who was a Baptist, those liberal sentiments which he ultimately embodied in the basis of the State

* See Washington's Reply to Memorial of Virginian Baptists, and Dr. Howell's History of Virginian Baptists.

bearing his name? And, as we have already seen, several of the master spirits in our political independence, and in the founding of our civil government, were in the closest contact at the outset of our struggles with Virginian Baptist ministers, whose souls were penetrated with these great interests, and the first of whose enthusiasm could not but have its influence.

Another well-known fact must be taken into account. There was a small Baptist Church, which held its monthly meetings for business, at a short distance from Mr. Jefferson's house, eight or ten years before the American Revolution. Mr. Jefferson was accustomed to attend these meetings. The pastor, on one occasion, asked him how he was pleased with their church government?

Mr. Jefferson replied, that it struck him with great force, and had interested him much; *that he considered it the only form of true democracy then existing in the world,* and had concluded that it would be the *best plan of government for the American colonies.*

It is also a fact, capable of abundant proof, that Mr. Jefferson was accustomed freely to confess to his associates, that the Baptist doctrines on that subject had enlightened and fixed his principles in relation to religious freedom.* Who can doubt, therefore, the source of those principles of *civil* freedom and equality which Mr. Jefferson afterwards so ably developed and advocated? Moreover, it is interesting here to note that, in the early controversies in the mother country respecting the proper treatment of the American colonies,

* See Howell's History of Viriginian Bapt. 93, and Curtis' Pro. Bap. Prin.

the English *Baptists* stood up in their defence, even when England was carrying on the war; and that, too, after Lord Chatham had deserted the cause of the colonies. Mention may be made in illustration of the thrilling words of Dr. John Ryland, as to the then existing struggle for Independence, in his conversation with Robert Hall, who was deeply penetrated with their justice and power.*

It should also be borne in mind, that sentiments of *religious* liberty cannot but beget and foster sentiments of *civil* liberty.

But not to insist upon this obligation respecting civil liberty, it is enough, that the Baptists have been honored by God, as His chief instruments, in setting forth in different ages, the true idea of SOUL-LIBERTY, and in fighting the battles for its practical realization.

And now, reader, how sacred the trust, of those who come into possession of privileges so dearly bought!

---

* "Brother Hall, I will tell you what I would do if I were General Washington." "Well, what would you do?" "Why, Brother Hall, if I were Washington, I would summon all the American officers; they should form a circle around me, and I would address them, and we would offer a libation in our blood, and I would order one of them to bring a lancet and a punch-bowl, and he should bleed us all, one by one, into this punch-bowl, and I would be the first to bare my arm; and when the punch-bowl was full, and we had all been bled, I would call upon every man to consecrate himself to the work, by dipping his sword into the bowl, and entering into a solemn covenant engagement by oath, one to another; and we would swear by HIM that sits upon the throne, and liveth for ever and ever, that we would never sheath our swords while there was an English soldier in arms remaining in America! *That* is what I would do, Brother Hall."

With what concern, should we guard and perpetuate them? Our fathers sowed in tears, that we might reap in joy. Far be it from us to be unmindful of their virtues and achievements.

> "All holy memories, and sublime,
> And glorious, round us throng."

As some one has remarked, "Without a strong regard to their history, and the principles of their ancestors, a denomination may quite lose sight of those distinctive peculiarities which have been the source of its usefulness." The annals of our Baptist fathers, were annals of heroic martyrdom, through long and tedious years. Fined, imprisoned, despoiled of their goods, they suffered and endured, that we might enter into their labors. Let us prove ourselves worthy to inherit the legacy which they have bequeathed. Let us stand firm to the same principles. Not as bigots, but as lovers of the truth, let us adhere to those doctrines which were dear to their hearts.

Who would be ashamed of their peculiar tenets, or deem them no longer important? The mission of this people is not yet accomplished. Said the great Neander—"You, Baptists, will have a future." Who can doubt it? Rightly spake that eloquent martyr already referred to—Hubmeyer, *"I believe and know that Christendom will not receive its rising aright, till Baptism and the Lord's Supper, are restored to their original purity."* And for our cheer in the battle for whatsoever is right, the glorious words of this same old spiritual hero come down to us with the voice of a clarion: "Divine truth is immortal. It may perhaps, for long, be bound, scourged, crowned, crucified, and for a season be entombed in the grave; but on the third day, it shall rise again victorious, and rule and triumph for ever!"

And may God grant, that being permitted to worship him unrestrained, *your* worship, dear reader, may be pure and spiritual; that so it may be perpetuated around His throne for ever!

THE END.

A
BIOGRAPHICAL SKETCH
OF
HENRY CLAY FISH
(1820-1877)

BY

JOHN FRANKLIN JONES

A
BIOGRAPHICAL SKETCH
OF
HENRY CLAY FISH
(1820-1877)

enry Clay Fish was born in Halifax, Vermont, January 27, 1820 (Cathcart). Samuel Fish, the boy's father, was a pastor of the Baptist church in his home town for forty-plus years. In 1836 and at age sixteen, the younger Fish united with his father's church (Griffiths, 296-98). The young Fish completed high school work at Halifax and at the Shelburn Falls Academy (Cathcart).

Fish came to New Jersey in 1840 and taught for two years. Impressed that he ought to preach, he entered Union Theological Seminary in 1842 and graduated in 1845. On June 26, 1845—the day following his graduation—he was ordained pastor at Somerville. That church prospered during the five years of his labors thereat (Griffiths).

First, Newark called him and Fish became pastor there in January, 1851. His nearly twenty-seven years of service at that church were exceedingly blessed. The church enjoyed great revivals (1854, 1858, 1864, 1866, 1876) and significant ingatherings (numbering 106, 236, 125, 152, 224, respectively). During his tenure, more than fourteen hundred were baptized. Church membership increased from 340 to 1199 (Griffiths).

The churches in Newark benefited greatly from Fish's ministry. He was influential in the number of churches increasing from three Baptist churches in Newark to ten and from a composite membership of 535 to 3055 (Griffiths).

Fish's church was a center of patriotic interest during the Civil War (1861-65). The location of many mass meetings, one hundred and seventy-two from among its members and congregation enlisted in the armies. Even the pastor was drafted, but the church sent a substitute in his place (Griffiths).

Fish gave a large place to the denominational and educational interests of New Jersey.

The secretary of the New Jersey Education Society for twenty-three years, he was primary in founding the German department of Rochester University (Griffiths). The University of Rochester conferred upon him the degree of D.D. (Cathcart). He labored for the Denominational schools. The last twelve years of his life saw him devotedly befriending Peddie Institute (Griffiths). His promotion of education stimulated an interest among the churches in the ministry and in ministerial education (Cathcart).

In July, 1877, Fish's physical condition brought to an end his full activities. Regarding his approaching passing and in his last hours, he said, "Don't say death...I shall soon be on the other side. H.C. Fish is nothing; the grace of God is everything." He left instructions for his funeral: "Let it be a plan of victory, the shout of him that overcometh through the Blood of the Lamb." Attending his death, his friends caught his broken, passing words: "I have fought." He died October 3, 1877, fifty-eight years of age (Griffiths).

Reports circulated that ten thousand people viewed his remains. One-hundred-plus clergymen attended the burial. During his lifetime, Fish preached over four thousand sermons/addresses, made twenty thousand visits (Griffiths), and made wide use of printed tracts (many self-composed) (Cathcart).

Fish wrote busily. Among his works were prize essays, frequent newspaper, and religious press articles (Griffiths, 296-98). He authored several books, publishing an average of one volume each of twenty years. Among those works are *Primitive Piety, Primitive Piety Revived, The History and Repository of Pulpit Eloquence, Pulpit Eloquence of the Nineteenth Century,*

The Handbook of Revivals, The American Manual of Life Insurance, Bible Lands Illustrated (the result of an eight-month journey abroad in 1874) (Cathcart), and *The Price of Soul Liberty and Who Paid It.*

BIBLIOGRAPHY

Cathcart, William, ed. *The Baptist Encyclopædia: A Dictionary of the Doctrines, Ordinances, Usages, Confessions of Faith, Sufferings, Labors, and Successes, and of the General History of the Baptist Denomination in All Lands, with Numerous Biographical Sketches of Distinguished American and Foreign Baptist, and a Supplement.* Philadelphia, Louis H. Everts, 1881; reprint, Paris, AR: Baptist Standard Bearer, 1988. S.v. "Fish, Henry Clay, D.D."

Fish, Henry Clay. *The Price of Soul Liberty and Who Paid It.* Boston: Sheldon & Co. and New York: Gould and Lincoln, 1860.

Griffiths, Thomas S. *A History of Baptists in New Jersey.* CD-Rom Version 1.0 in *The Baptist History Collection, Ages Software.* Paris, AR: Baptist Standard Bearer, 2005.

John Franklin Jones
Cordova, Tennessee
January 2008

THE BAPTIST STANDARD BEARER, INC.

a non-profit, tax-exempt corporation
committed to the Publication & Preservation
of the Baptist Heritage.

———◆———

CURRENT TITLES AVAILABLE IN
THE BAPTIST *DISTINCTIVES* SERIES

CARSON, ALEXANDER — Ecclesiastical Polity of the New Testament. (Dublin: William Carson, 1856).

BOOTH, ABRAHAM — A Defense of the Baptists. A Declaration and Vindication of Three Historically Distinctive Baptist Principles. Compiled and Set Forth in the Republication of Three Books. Revised edition. (Paris, AR: The Baptist Standard Bearer, Inc., 2006).

BOOTH, ABRAHAM — Paedobaptism Examined on the Principles, Concessions, and Reasonings of the Most Learned Paedobaptists. With Replies to the Arguments and Objections of Dr. Williams and Mr. Peter Edwards. 3 volumes. (London: Ebenezer Palmer, 1829).

CARROLL, B. H. — *Ecclesia* - The Church. With an Appendix. (Louisville: Baptist Book Concern, 1903).

CHRISTIAN, JOHN T. — Immersion, The Act of Christian Baptism. (Louisville: Baptist Book Concern, 1891).

FROST, J. M. — Pedobaptism: Is It From Heaven Or Of Men? (Philadelphia: American Baptist Publication Society, 1875).

FULLER, RICHARD — Baptism, and the Terms of Communion; An Argument. (Charleston, SC: Southern Baptist Publication Society, 1854).

GRAVES, J. R. — Tri-Lemma: or, Death By Three Horns. The Presbyterian General Assembly Not Able To Decide This Question: "Is Baptism In The Romish Church Valid?" 1st Edition.

(Nashville: Southwestern Publishing House, 1861).

MELL, P.H.   Baptism In Its Mode and Subjects. (Charleston, SC: Southern Baptist Publications Society, 1853).

JETER, JEREMIAH B.   Baptist Principles Reset. Consisting of Articles on Distinctive Baptist Principles by Various Authors. With an Appendix. (Richmond: The Religious Herald Co., 1902).

PENDLETON, J.M.   Distinctive Principles of Baptists. (Philadelphia: American Baptist Publication Society, 1882).

THOMAS, JESSE B.   The Church and the Kingdom. A New Testament Study. (Louisville: Baptist Book Concern, 1914).

WALLER, JOHN L.   Open Communion Shown to be Unscriptural & Deleterious. With an introductory essay by Dr. D. R. Campbell and an Appendix. (Louisville: Baptist Book Concern, 1859).

For a complete list of current authors/titles, visit our internet site at:
www.standardbearer.org
or write us at:

he Baptist Standard Bearer, Inc.

NUMBER ONE IRON OAKS DRIVE • PARIS, ARKANSAS 72855

TEL # 479-963-3831   FAX # 479-963-8083
EMAIL: Baptist@centurytel.net   http://www.standardbearer.org

Thou hast given a standard to them that fear thee; that it may be displayed because of the truth. — Psalm 60:4

www.ingramcontent.com/pod-product-compliance
Lightning Source LLC
Chambersburg PA
CBHW022119280326
41933CB00007B/454